Raising
Gifted Children

Raising
Gifted
Children

A Practical Guide for Parents Facing Big Emotions and Big Potential

Catherine Zakoian, MA, NCC, LPC

ROCKRIDGE
PRESS

Interior and Cover Designer: Richard Tapp
Art Producer: Janice Ackerman
Editor: Mo Mozuch

Cover Illustration: toffu.com.
Interior Illustration Courtesy of Shutterstock.

ISBN: Print 978-1-64739-629-9 | eBook 978-1-64739-630-5
R0

"If there is anything that we wish to change in the child, we should first examine it and see whether it is not something that could better be changed in ourselves."—Carl Jung (1939)

Contents

Foreword

Growing up my parents didn't know what to make of me, my idiosyncrasies, the way I processed the world, my interest in peculiar things. If my parents had seen this book when I was in school they would have walked right past it, because I am neither gifted nor talented.

This book is for the parents of gifted children and the ones who are just discovering their child may be gifted and have no idea what to do next. It gives those parents (not mine) practical guidance and strategies for dealing with the everyday intensity, perceptivity, sensitivity, and perfectionism of their child.

As I said before, I, myself, not gifted—but Catherine is, and she has written a clear guide of how to proceed in the world of the "gifted" child. As I have said many, many times, I, myself, am not gifted. But I have seen a great deal of gifted and talented people in my time at *Saturday Night Live* and this guide would certainly have helped them.

Good luck on your journey and with this guide. You're off to a good start.

Steve Higgins
Paris, 1928
(I'm not in Paris)
(Nor is it 1928)

Introduction

For the past 20 years, I have had the pleasure to work as a counselor and consultant in private practice with gifted, profoundly gifted, and twice-exceptional (2e) children, adolescents, teens, adults, couples, families, and organizations. I first decided to study counseling psychology while working in human resources management within creative entrepreneurial businesses. I wanted to better understand how to support creative adults who had tremendous gifts but (rightly) struggled with how to stay true to their vision and themselves, yet flourish in everyday life. I am gifted myself, so I know these challenges firsthand.

My graduate program was, and continues to be, accredited and highly regarded, and the mix of researchers and practitioners were perfect for my development as an integrated clinician. The summer before my internship began, I registered for a course in counseling children and families. Many of my classmates planned to work with children; I did not. Yet I discovered, with the help of my excellent professor, working with children and families was an exceptionally good match for my nature and skill set, so I changed direction.

In my yearlong internship, I worked at a large regional mental health center in one of the most beautiful parts of Colorado's Rocky Mountains. Under a grant, and alongside my brilliant clinical supervisor, I provided in-home family therapy services to families who were heading toward "out-of-home placement" for their children. In other words, if dynamics didn't change these families were close to being broken up at some level by the child welfare authority. Despite the gravity of the situation, each family had just 12 sessions with us to sort out what they wished to create for themselves and to develop a plan to work in that direction. I learned to work quickly and creatively, and to balance the tension with kindhearted lightness. Together, alongside these excellent and well-meaning families, we compassionately untangled their challenges and nurtured their strengths.

I have since counseled large numbers of gifted individuals, helping them find calm, authenticity, and harmony. As an educational consultant, I have created meaningful social-emotional and educational programming for gifted children, teens, and parents, and broadened the awareness of giftedness among early childhood, elementary, and secondary educators and administrators. I have worked with many public, independent, and alternative schools to create better environments for both gifted and neurotypical students and educators. I co-created a groundbreaking kindergarten readiness project at a diverse, historic preschool. I assisted in the development of an alternative high school program for at risk gifted, twice-exceptional, and neurotypical teens, helping to steer them from the brink of marginalization, underachievement, and drop-out toward brighter futures.

Wherever I work as a consultant, I often spot gifted or twice-exceptional children who have yet to be identified, or have been misidentified, and are typically perceived as troublesome. I am proud of this work illuminating and supporting unrecognized brilliance, because it seems to be one way to offset our social and educational systems that can miss, then misunderstand, and later marginalize these children and families.

Working well and effectively with a gifted population takes a great deal of energy and range. I know parenting or teaching gifted children can be difficult, but I also know that almost any circumstance, no matter how serious, can be addressed wisely, kindheartedly, and from a strengths perspective. While this may seem overwhelming, know that there are understandings, reflections, tools, and practices you can develop that can open the window and bring light and fresh air in to your parenting journey to lessen the challenge and increase the delight of raising brilliant children.

I was asked to write this book from the perspective of my clinical expertise, to help people just starting the journey of understanding giftedness. I hope you find my practical guidance valuable and helpful as you parent and otherwise serve the gifted children in your life.

How to Use This Book

This book is designed with care to be an accessible primer in parenting gifted children. We will begin with a brief foundational overview of giftedness, then explore characteristics and dynamics of giftedness before outlining practical ways to support gifted children in their development at home, socially, and in school.

I will offer you a good starting point in these pages. And within that information, I have referenced and cited many excellent contributors, researchers, and practitioners in the field to point you in their directions when you are ready to take your understanding of giftedness further. In addition to these reference points, you will find a gifted resources section at the end of this book for your use as well.

As a counselor, my approach to working with gifted people is anchored in the social-emotional, mental health, and well-being realms of this discussion. I stay open to and explore the variety of voices, research, ideas, and professional approaches that examine and define the field, yet my work is authentic, innovative, and informed by my own training, education, and experience. As a practitioner, I don't nearsightedly follow along with the consensus opinions. This autonomous and divergent stance allows me to be more genuinely aligned to support the health and development of the brilliant, independent-thinking gifted children, adolescents, teens, and adults I serve.

In reading my book, I suggest you do the same: I encourage you to stay true to yourself. Take what works for you and leave the rest. Find your own way, be authentic in your parenting, and, if in reading my book you find your parenting path, philosophies, policies or practices broaden or shift, embrace the change.

A Note about Research

I have been fortunate to find my way to work that is meaningful for me and is helpful to children and families. I am doubly blessed to work in a profession offering lineage and the legacy of a verbal tradition. In addition to my graduate work preparaton, I have regularly and intentionally sat with and learned from wise counselors before me throughout the many years I have been practicing. Through this ongoing dialogue and reflection I have learned from the ancestors, so to speak, of counseling, psychology, education, and giftedness (and the ancestors before them, and the ancestors before them . . .).

Much effort has been made to provide citations for any concepts that are not my own. This includes robust reference and resource lists for parents who may wish to dive further into the work surrounding giftedness as well as citations throughout the book. The aim is to acknowledge the many minds and many ideas that have shaped this field, or my approach to this field, and give proper credit to those whose work has proven invaluable. Please forgive me if I have missed acknowledging someone; it was not intentional.

CHAPTER ONE

What We Mean When We Say Gifted

This chapter offers a look at the different perspectives and ideas on how to define the gifted child, to give you an understanding of how your child may be viewed by schools, counselors, and other related practitioners—although in some places you may find there is little awareness of giftedness at all. There is much to explore in this realm, and some concepts may seem at odds with other ideas. For some people, especially some gifted people, starting here can paradoxically feel burdensome and disconnected from their over- all interest in the topic—in this case, parenting gifted children well. If you feel this way, skip this chapter for now and trust you will know when returning to explore this beginning material makes sense for you.

How We Define Gifted

As you start this process of understanding your gifted child and begin to sift through definitions, resources, and conversations, I advise you again to become clear on what feels right to you. If your child was identified as gifted in a school setting, consider broadening this understanding by seeking out a consultation or a privately administered evaluation. An experienced evaluator, deeply specialized in giftedness and twice-exceptionality (2e, see page 16), can better see and understand within and beyond the test process indicators of potential twice-exceptionality. Such an assessment can paint a fuller picture of your child's learning needs, strengths, and challenges, all of which will most likely benefit from the earliest intervention and will support your child properly into their adulthood.

Do your homework on this step; it is an expensive process and you only want to work with the best. Evaluators can come from various paths including educational psychology, neuropsychology, and clinical psychology. Sadly, psychology training programs often do not include much, if any, preparation in giftedness or twice-exceptionality. As a result, practitioners who are deeply skilled in evaluating giftedness can be difficult to find.

I'd advise you to consider the following:

▶ The experience of the evaluator is critical! Be assertive and ask the evaluator to outline their direct experience with, training in, and understanding of evaluating gifted children and learning differences. Here are a few questions to ask: How long have you worked with gifted children? How many gifted or twice-exceptional children have you evaluated? How do you discern signs of possible twice-exceptionality?

▶ Ask for and contact references.

- Do not be shy to ask each evaluator to explain their training and experience in understanding and evaluating giftedness, learning differences, and twice-exceptionality.
- As you are interviewing evaluators, try to include practitioners who come out of the field of educational psychology.
- Find an organization that focuses solely on gifted evaluation with an understanding of twice-exceptionality versus gifted educational consulting outfits or gifted tutoring groups that farm out assessments to psychologists without a primary specialization in giftedness. These middleman services can seem to be good value, but can lead to problems like depressed scores, misdiagnoses, and missed opportunities to identify and support a hidden learning or processing challenge.
- Understand you may have to travel to find the right assessment resource.

There are many misconceptions, definitions, strong opinions, intense emotions, and varied responses surrounding what it means for a child to be gifted. There are important varying definitions to consider. As a parent of a gifted child just beginning the gifted journey, it is common to feel overwhelmed and isolated as you search out resources, navigate conversations with family members, and attempt to advocate for your child. You are not alone! Part of what you are experiencing is confusion within the field itself.

How Giftedness Is Expressed

A long-standing and ongoing tension exists within the greater gifted field between the idea that giftedness and talent should translate to high achievement, and the idea that giftedness is an inner experience to be nurtured holistically in order to properly develop (Silverman 2013a). Often our education system, mental health system, and family systems can get tangled in this same argument, tragically leaving in the wake the incorrect idea that only high-achieving children at the top of a classroom are gifted.

This is only the tip of the iceberg regarding giftedness and gifted identification. Layered into this systemic dispute, we see schools work hard to identify and support gifted children, yet still often miss identifying gifted children beyond classroom performance. There are gifted children who are spirited and will not comply or be obedient to authority. There are creative children who think divergently (Betts and Neihart 1988, 2010) and bright children who find school meaningless and disengage (Delisle 2018). There are perfectionistic children who hang back or underachieve as a coping strategy, or twice-exceptional children who have simultaneous identified or unidentified learning or processing challenges that may eclipse their gifted strengths (Mooney and Cole 2000). This is also true for culturally diverse children who are not yet fully seen (Plucker, Burroughs, et al. 2010); English language learners who are not yet fully heard; traumatized children living in neglectful, abusive, or addicted family systems (Perfect, Turley, et al. 2016; Perry 2002); or children living with challenges like environmental toxicity or food and nutrition concerns (Washington 2019) that keep them from being their best.

Further compounding this puzzle is the reality that most gifted children, like gifted adults, are intense, sensitive, perfectionistic, keenly perceptive, and uneven in their development. This nuanced combination of characteristics can lead parents and educators to incorrect conclusions about perceived pathology, misbehavior, and social-emotional deficits within the classroom, family, and other social settings. These misperceptions leave gifted children unsupported in their learning, in parts of their lives, and in their development because they are often mislabeled, misplaced, isolated, marginalized, and misunderstood.

A BRIEF HISTORY OF DEFINING "GIFTED"

Essentially, giftedness means high cognitive ability. Yet giftedness is much more than can be described as high cognitive ability. It can be a helpful exercise to familiarize yourself with the variety and development of definitions of giftedness. You will most likely be your child's primary advocate, so having a grounding in giftedness at this level can help you prepare for all of the ways giftedness is perceived, understood, and described. Following is a handful of sources of varying and compelling definitions you may wish to explore:

The Marland Report (1972)

The first national report on gifted education was prepared and presented to Congress by Sydney P. Marland, United States Commissioner of Education. Marland's definition of giftedness is notable because he essentially advocated for specialized education and went on to describe the social-emotional pitfalls of not properly supporting these learners. He also delineated areas of giftedness within the context of education. It reads, in part:

> *Gifted and talented children are those identified by professionally qualified persons who, by virtue of outstanding abilities, are capable of high performance. These are children who require differentiated educational programs and/or services beyond those normally provided by the regular school program in order to realize their contribution to self and society.*
>
> *Children capable of high performance include those with demonstrated achievement and/or potential ability in any of the following areas, singularly or in combination:*

- *General Intellectual Ability;*
- *Specific Academic Aptitude;*
- *Creative or Productive Thinking;*
- *Leadership Ability;*
- *Visual and Performing Arts Ability; or*
- *Psychomotor Ability* (Marland 1972)

Annemarie Roeper (1982)

The daughter of progressive educators, Annemarie Roeper (with her husband George) founded what has become the oldest independent school for the gifted in the United States, the Roeper School in Michigan. She emphasized the emotional or inner experience of giftedness in her definition: *"[A] greater awareness, a greater sensitivity, and a greater ability to understand and transform perceptions into intellectual and emotional experiences."* (Roeper 1982)

Joseph Renzulli (1986)

Joseph Renzulli is a researcher, professor, and educational psychologist who conceptualized giftedness within a frame of human and creative potential. He related it to behavior and environment within a model comprised of three interlocking rings of above-average ability, creativity, and task commitment (Renzulli 2005).

The Columbus Group (1991)

The Columbus Group, a collegial circle of deeply experienced gifted practitioners, researchers, authors, and educators, developed a beautifully holistic definition that also underlined the term "asynchrony," which essentially refers to uneven development (Silverman 1992, 1993, 1997, 2013a, 2013b, [in press]; eds. Neville, Piechowski, et al. 2013). For more on asynchrony, see page 35.

"Giftedness is asynchronous development in which advanced cognitive abilities and heightened intensity combine to create inner experiences and awareness that are qualitatively different from the norm. This asynchrony increases with higher intellectual capacity. The uniqueness of the gifted renders them particularly vulnerable and requires modifications in parenting, teaching, and counseling in order for them to develop optimally."

National Association for Gifted Children (2019)

The National Association for Gifted Children, a power-house education and advocacy organization, recently revised their definition to highlight the comparative performance capacity of gifted students, requiring modified education to realize potential. They go on to underscore the diversity of gifted students as well as highlight the needs of gifted students, including access, intervention and accommodation, social-emotional support and guidance, and related services (NAGC 2019).

Domains of Giftedness

Initially, many parents, like many people, think of giftedness as involving academic strengths. They might picture a gifted child as a high-achiever earning top grades at the top of the class. While there are certainly gifted kids who fit this description, high achievement and academic success are far from the only indicators and measures of giftedness. The domains of giftedness outlined here stem from the current federal definition of giftedness from the Elementary and Secondary Education Act, which were birthed originally from The Marland Report (see page 5).

"The term 'gifted and talented,' when used with respect to students, children, or youth, means students, children, or youth who give evidence of high achievement capability in such areas of intellectual, creative, artistic, or leadership capacity, or in specific academic fields, and who need services or activities not ordinarily provided by the school in order to fully develop those capabilities" (No Child Left Behind 2001).

These domains are:

- Intellectual
- Academic
- Creative
- Leadership
- Artistic

In my work, and within collegial circles, there are other realms of giftedness that can be seen. Three of these areas are:

- Emotional
- Social/Relational
- Spiritual

As a parent, it is helpful to provide your child access and opportunity to develop their interests and talents in different domains. Your child's contributions to the world, and their happiness, may certainly live outside of traditional education. Track and support what seems to interest your child, even if it is vastly different from what you expected, or your or your family's interests and capacities.

Based on my areas of expertise, here are my under-standings of each domain along with a few ideas to support development in these areas.

Intellectual

Sometimes this domain overlaps with school, but most often children, adolescents, teens, and adults who are intellectu-ally gifted need to delve into specific and far-reaching areas of intellectual interest that are of sincere personal interest beyond their school curriculum. They want and need to think and explore deeply.

As a parent, I recommend you set up a regular, ongoing meeting with your child to discuss what is currently interesting to them and put together resources and access to materials as best you can to support their curiosity. I suggest loosely structuring this meeting as a humorous research proposal exchange. Your child brings the ideas, needs, and budget requests. You provide the hot chocolate and try to stay open to their thoughts, no matter how grand or fantastical. Work together to find ways to support their ideas and set project guidelines for safety. Explain from the beginning, before you even sit down, that not everything they request may be possible, but you commit to giving each idea your time and consideration, and there is the possibility that projects may need to be redeveloped. When you do need to reconsider an idea, follow up with your child as you promised.

This does not necessarily need to be an expensive venture, nor would I recommend you invest heavily in equipment and resources, as a gifted child may put down an area of focus quickly as they move on to their next interest. For example, a child who is interested in ancient astronomy may dream of a field trip to Stonehenge, but you can start instead with a borrowed telescope, a trip to the observatory, and a month of Saturdays of popcorn and documentaries.

Finding and vetting mentors for your child is another way to help them access expertise. I have seen this accomplished well via regular in-person and/or video chat meetings. Don't be hesitant to advocate for your child and reach out to people you think could be a helpful influence. You can also include your child in the process of finding a potential mentor by scribing a brief statement or list of what they wish to learn and accomplish that you can communicate with the potential mentor.

Academic

Different gifted children may excel in different academic areas such as math or language arts. Because gifted children have varied academic strengths, challenges, interests, and skills (see Asynchrony, page 35), you might also see varied outcomes across different subjects. For example, a child may be showing advanced skill in language arts but not in another area like math.

Parents may need to supplement a child's education to meet their child's interests and academic development. Tutors can be helpful if they are a good match with your child's nature and learning style (see Two Learning Styles, page 20). In my experience, extra work like this is most productive if it is kept fun and engaging for the child.

Creative

These are the young people who can be excellent problem-solvers and innovators—sometimes builders, sometimes not. They generally need, like those in the intellectual domain, regular reflection on their ideas and interests, as well as access to materials and resources. Often these young people may struggle to enjoy school from year to year, depending on program and educator fit.

This domain can be difficult to appreciate. These gifted children and adolescents will be excellent problem-solvers, but they may not appear this way to their parents or educators, who may experience them as disruptive, unorganized, or unable to keep their desks tidy.

Artistic

This domain encompasses music, dance, studio, and other fine arts, and, like creativity, can be hard to spot. Yes, some traditional manifestations will be obvious, like a child who can draw well and realistically, or a musical teen who can flawlessly perform composed classical music. But there are many children who aren't as easy to figure out—for example, young children who write poetic country music lyrics or teens engaged in street art—and trying to compare artistic capacity to traditional measures of talent is like comparing apples and oranges. These children benefit from exploration, instruction, and mentorship in the areas of their interests.

Perfectionism can be a challenge for these children, stopping them cold in their creativity as they compare what they wish to create with the beginning stages of their work, or they inaccurately compare their skill against someone else (we delve more into perfectionism on page 30). In my experience, it is helpful to show young gifted children a variety of creative expressions and techniques so they can move more easily past their perfectionism and find their own creative way—for example, discussing the differences between a painter like Georgia O'Keeffe and a painter like Mark Rothko, and wondering what it might look like if one tried to paint like the other.

Work to find school settings and other art, dance, writing, and music teachers that focus on creative expression, composition freedom, and process in addition to technique rather than outcome-based instruction focused only on technical quality and finished product and works. Children who move into fine arts paths will have time to hone technical skills to complement their love of these areas.

If your child is interested, set up a home studio space for them. It doesn't need to be large, have a ballet barre, or be acoustically balanced, well-furnished, or perfectly lit—just a spot where they know they can work on what they love without concern about making a mess. Discuss with them in advance what furnishings and supplies make sense (for art studios, some children find recyclable materials wonderful to work with) and let them help you put it all together. Ideally, it is a spot that does not need to be used for another family purpose and can remain as their workspace.

Leadership

Traditionally this domain was reserved for students who stepped into activities and responsibilities at school and beyond. In my experience, you can sometimes broaden this domain parameter to include gifted people who tend to take a stand for the underdog and everyday injustices, although this is not always the case. If your child's giftedness shows up in this domain, they will benefit from your support and regular reflection.

It can be helpful to give them access to biographies of other leaders, although I caution you to find true biographies as opposed to glossed-over textbook histories that omit much of the story that your child will identify with and benefit from learning. Also, access to works on philosophy, especially in politics and society, can be helpful.

Emotional

Gifted people can be acutely empathic. In addition to their own deep wells of emotional experience, they can sometimes sense and feel the emotional experiences of others. Some of the children I work with are so tuned to others they can become caught up in a confusion of what are their feelings and what belongs to others. On a larger scale, these children can be deeply attuned to the pain of the community or world around them and sometimes wish and work to address it. Gifted scholar Michael Piechowski (2003) describes:

> *"Emotional giftedness finds expression in helping others when no one else would, alleviating distress, opposing unfairness, and fighting injustice."*

These young people can benefit from regular, ongoing daily reflection and conversation with adults they can trust about their experiences. For children who are affected by others' feelings, help them become aware of this through reflective conversation. You can also support an emotionally gifted child in exploring ways to be of service that are meaningful to them.

In chapter 3 we will discuss how you can also help your empathic child by becoming aware of your own feelings. We will also discuss how to reflect for your gifted child.

Social or Relational

Many gifted children experience awkwardness and a variety of social dilemmas as they seek connection and friendship (see chapter 6). For others, this is not the case. These children have a natural capacity for initiating authentic connection and genuinely befriending others. They can often read the social landscape of their environments and describe it concisely to you.

One challenge I see in my practice regarding this domain is when these children, although social, are also introverted. They need alone time to recharge. Sometimes they prefer one-on-one time with friends instead of constant group activities even at school, so they may require your assistance to find balance. We will discuss these and other dynamics more in chapter 3.

Another more common challenge can occur when gifted children, teens, and adults—especially girls and women—are able to adapt themselves to match up with people, befriending them easily and creating connection based on likeness. When these connections require the gifted person to modify who they are to fit in, they are essentially living inauthentically and this can and will take a toll. If you do this yourself, working to shift into authenticity, being true to yourself, will enable your child to do the same.

Spiritual

This area is hard to define narrowly. It is not necessarily an interest in religion, although it could be. It also can be a sense of connection with nature or with the whole of humanity. Some of the children I work with report extraordinary experiences, for example, relating to their connection to deceased family members. It can be many other phenomena as well. Psychologist Deirdre Lovecky (1998) calls this *spiritual sensitivity in gifted children*:

> *These children understand the universality of spiritual concepts such as forgiveness of others ... develop a systemic philosophy of life and death, or are seekers of the transcendent in the universe, other people, and themselves.*

Sometimes these children will talk directly with their parents about their experiences and ideas. These children can sense when their parents, other family members, or friends don't share their experiences. When this happens a gifted child is at risk of hiding this sensibility from others, potentially creating an experience of loneliness or isolation.

It can be beneficial for parents of these children to acknowledge their child's nature without judgment or fear. They should offer to be a place of support and reflection even if they do not share the same experiences or understand this sensibility (see chapter 3).

It is also beneficial for parents not to impose their own beliefs in this area on their children. It is certainly fine to discuss and share, but once there is an expectation that a child must be a certain way, the authentic line of communication between parent and child around these matters can close.

A Gifted IQ

Intelligence tests were developed to measure intelligence or cognitive ability. A child's scores represent where they land in various ways on overall ability and subtest scores. The levels of what is considered giftedness start at about two standard deviations above the norm (of 100) at around 130 and rise from there into the highly gifted, exceptionally gifted, and profoundly gifted ranges.

In school settings, achievement tests and IQ tests (or both) are used to evaluate children. IQ tests are *cognitive ability* tests and vary in objective from *achievement* tests, which measure what a student has learned already. Schools often test individual children using group methods meant for measuring progression and will sometimes universally screen for inclusion in gifted programs, though not always. School screening is often how parents discover their child's giftedness, but as achievement measures are generally not designed to identify giftedness, they cannot necessarily determine the level of a child's giftedness (Silverman 2018).

Further complicating matters, some domains of giftedness, like creativity, are not evaluated using these types of methods. These tests can frequently miss undiagnosed twice-exceptional children, thus excluding them from gifted programing that may have been beneficial.

English language learners are also among the populations that can be missed in the school evaluation process, although there are efforts in the field to identify these children and children experiencing other inequities more effectively. Although IQ testing contributes to identifying and understanding a child's advanced cognitive capacity, and certain IQ scores quantify above-average cognitive ability or giftedness, these measures do not *define* giftedness, which is a much richer inner experience and collection of unique individual capacities.

WHAT IS TWICE-EXCEPTIONALITY (2E) OR MULTI-EXCEPTIONALITY?

Twice-exceptionality (2e) means that in addition to having the gifted exceptionality of advanced cognitive ability, the individual also has a second exceptionality (or, for multi-exceptionality, multiple exceptionalities) in their makeup. Exceptionalities are learning, processing, or other related challenges like dyslexia, dysgraphia (difficulty writing), sensory processing or integration concerns, autism, visual processing challenges, or auditory processing concerns like central auditory processing disorder. Physical and emotional challenges are also considered exceptionalities. Once identified and well supported, these differences typically become assets for gifted people as they allow these individuals to experience the world in unique ways, leading to massively creative thinking, contribution, and innovation. This level of neurodiversity is tremendous, but can be easily missed and misunderstood.

Undiagnosed twice- or multi-exceptional children frequently make their way in early elementary school because their giftedness can, for a short time, outpace the demands of the classroom. However, at some point twice-exceptional children hit a wall in their learning and academic functioning. If this occurs in middle school or beyond, the child will experience the double dilemma of not having developed study habits along the way because they didn't need to study in the earlier years. This dilemma can spiral into emotional distress as well as self-worth and self-safety concerns. Parents need not rush out tomorrow morning and double down on developing traditional study habits in their gifted children; in chapter 4, I will give you more context and strategy on how to support your child's natural inclination toward learning.

You want to do all you can as a parent to watch for and address twice- or multi-exceptionality because it can be an exhausting and difficult way to go through life. This is a tall order because parents can unknowingly possess the same exceptionalities and have learned to live with them, hence they cannot see it as a difference in their child. You also need to know what you are looking for, and it can be difficult to discern where to begin the process.

A good place to start in detecting challenges is paying attention to what your child avoids—follow these bread-crumbs to see where they might lead. For example:

- A child who avoids reading may benefit from a dyslexia evaluation. Or this child may have visual processing concerns, like their eyes do not track or work together, and a visit with a *developmental optometrist* (Kavner 1985) is merited. Note: This is a *different and more specialized* evaluation than an ordinary vision exam or screening through your optometrist or school.

- A child who misses or disregards verbal directions, or avoids or becomes agitated in noisy environments, may benefit from a *central auditory processing evaluation* (See Able Kids Foundation in Resources). Note: This is a *different and more specialized* evaluation than an ordinary hearing exam or screening through your pediatrician or school.

- Contacting a pediatric occupational therapist is generally a helpful step for children who are *sensory over-responsive, sensory under-responsive, or sensory craving* (Miller, Fuller, et al. 2007). For example, certain fabrics, or labels and seams in clothing are irritating and the child refuses to wear the items. Or children who do not notice when they are hurt and bleeding. Or children who will seek out excessive physical connection.

It is best to find practitioners who have solid experience with gifted children. This is easier said than done, even in locations that seem to offer a lot of options. Here's what I recommend to make things easier:

- Cast a wide net. Ask other parents of gifted children, if you can, and compile a list of recommendations.
- Find local, regional, or state gifted organizations and see if they have a resource list.
- Contact large gifted talent development programs serving gifted children.
- Ask university education departments if they offer any evaluation or clinic services, or if they can refer you to other departments, programs, or individuals.
- Check with the children's hospital in your region.
- Sometimes specialty parent groups on social media can offer ideas, but as you already know, if you go this route it may be best to ask generally and do not describe your child or your concerns in detail on a public platform.

You may need to garner several opinions or evaluations because a child has already developed some form of internal accommodation to override challenges, or because a child's intelligence and perfectionism can detect and outpace the short evaluation. It is also possible that you may need to travel to find the right evaluation and support.

Gifted Learner Profiles

I like to introduce George Betts and Maureen Neihart's work on gifted learner profiles (1988, 2010) to the children, teens, adults, and families I counsel, as well as to educators who seek to ground their understanding and support of gifted learners. These researchers describe six types of gifted learner profiles.

Their model generously gives us the feelings, attitudes, behaviors, needs, perceptions, and support ideas for each type. To help you get started, here are brief descriptions of each profile:

Successful

These students tend to be successful in school. They understand the system and work just enough to achieve good grades. There is a fear of failure, which can translate to not taking risks. These learners test well and are liked by teachers. These are the students who typically appear to teachers to be gifted in school and are placed in gifted programs. These learners can be at risk for later underachievement, as well as a diminished creative capacity and sense of autonomy.

Creative

These are tremendously creative learners who can have greater potential than what their teachers can see. They are divergent thinkers who tend to challenge the system, rules, and authority. They are often not identified as gifted as easily as some other profiles. These learners, if not supported early on, can be at risk for dropping out of school.

Underground

This learner prefers to fit in socially at school and wishes to hide their giftedness. This can be a change from an earlier gifted learning profile that was more engaged. Typically, this will occur in middle school for girls (Kerr 1985) and high school for boys, when a desire to belong may outweigh their academic pursuits.

At-Risk

This learner often emerges in high school, sometimes earlier. These students have experienced school as unhelpful and are at the point of anger. This can occur after years of having their abilities and interests go unrecognized and unsupported. This learner is at risk of dropping out.

Twice-exceptional/Multi-exceptional

This learning profile represents individuals who are both gifted and have a learning or processing difficulty, or another challenge, like autism, simultaneously. Sometimes these learners are erroneously seen as not gifted.

Autonomous

These learners are intrinsically motivated and can see failure as part of learning. They are self-confident, self-directed, creative, and able to problem-solve. Autonomous learners tend to care about humanity and view learning as a life pursuit.

Betts built on this work with others to formulate The Autonomous Learner Model (Betts and Kercher 1999) and subsequent resource supports (Betts, Carey, Kapushion 2016).

This work is straightforward and can help you better understand your gifted child and help them feel supported and understood within their learning development. Yet, as ever, there is complexity to consider. For example, it may sound like being a successful type of learner is optimal, however, there are potential pitfalls.

Two Learning Styles

In addition to understanding your gifted child's learner profile, I recommend you work to discover their learning style.

Put aside what you may have picked up along the way about learning styles and, for the purposes of parenting a gifted child, focus instead on two types: auditory-sequential learning and visual-spatial learning. The groundbreaking field of visual-spatial learning and the gifted learner was developed by gifted researcher and psychologist Linda Silverman whose book *Upside-Down Brilliance: The Visual Spatial Learner* is listed in the Resources section. Here is a brief sketch of each of these learning styles:

Auditory-Sequential Learning. Auditory-sequential learners prefer to learn in a step-by-step manner. School curriculum, materials, and teaching and classroom practices tend to be oriented toward the auditory-sequential learner as instruction moves students from basics to more depth. These learners' skills and natures are often well-matched with the school approach and seem to do quite well.

Visual-Spatial Learning. Visual-spatial learners prefer to learn the big concept first, and *then* go back to the details. Although teaching step-by-step seems an efficient way to coordinate classroom learning, when you are a visual-spatial learner this approach can lead you to believe that you are "not smart," or worse, "stupid." Paradoxically, visual-spatial learners can actually seek more complexity in their learning (Silverman 2002).

Without having this critical information, self-understanding, and subsequent academic modification and support, gifted children and teens can disengage at school, languish, decline, and potentially become at risk not only within their academics, but more tragically within their sense of self, self-efficacy, and self-worth. In my experience, once children are on this trajectory the risk can sometimes move far beyond their school engagement into the realm of self-safety.

I initiate this learning style conversation at my office and observe as children, teens, and adults who self-identify as visual-spatial learners can barely contain themselves as they explain that although they love to learn, parts—sometimes most—of the school learning experience can feel tedious and incomprehensible. We can connect these factors to some portion of their school disengagement, plan together to soften this learning disconnect, and work to authentically re-engage this learner through advocacy, work modification, and seeking better school fit.

Become clear about your own learning style. If you discover you are inclined toward one of these learning styles, and the child you parent or teach is inclined toward the other, you must develop awareness about how both styles can impact your connection and how you guide your child. This is especially true in a homeschool environment, as you assist children with their schoolwork, or in your process of obtaining learning support by selecting materials, hiring tutors, or arranging for participation in a learning program of any kind, even (and especially) within the creative arts.

I encourage you to explore the many, many comparisons and intricacies between the two learning styles in order to properly understand and advocate for your child's learning at school. Discuss this concept with your child as well.

Introverts and Extroverts

In his work on psychological types, renowned Swiss psychologist and theorist Carl Jung developed the terms introversion and extroversion (Jung 2014) to delineate tendencies he noticed in people. In essence, extroverts tend to find being with other people and in social settings, external time, to be energizing. Introverts tend to find alone time, internal time, to be energizing. It is completely possible to be social and introverted, but these introverts indeed need time alone to reenergize.

If, as introverts or extroverts, we go too long without having time to recharge we can start to emotionally falter, losing perspective and the harmony within ourselves and our relationships.

It is important for gifted families to determine who is an introvert or extrovert. If you are an introvert and your child is an extrovert, you will need to negotiate this together to allow for everyone to engage meaningfully in the world, recharge, and feel settled. Conversely, the same holds true if you have an introverted child and you are extroverted. You will need to help your child set up quiet ways for them to recharge, especially after a full day of school or other activity.

In my practice, I see families realize they are a mixture of both leanings, which frequently illuminates basic family disharmony. It is easily remedied as their awareness and practices grow in this area of family needs, planning, and functioning.

The Debate About Saying Gifted

Another conflict surrounding giftedness is in actually using the word "gifted" to describe children and academic programs. There appears to be sizeable misconception that erroneously translates giftedness to elitism or privilege. Systemic and individual misunderstanding can incorrectly view gifted children as possessing an endowment, that needs no supplemental resource or support. In this persistent, outdated view, gifted children can be tragically denied access to meaningful and necessary learning options and intervention.

I see a similar misunderstanding within family environments, sometimes between parents who are confused about the term but also concerned about labels, particularly if a parent had a difficult time with being identified, misidentified, or unidentified as gifted. Conflict frequently develops within extended family and friend communities, with those who misinterpret the meaning of giftedness, feel that a family is "bragging," or are uncomfortable as they compare their own child's development to the gifted child. A common refrain is "Aren't all children gifted?" Well, yes, all children have gifts. However, the term "gifted" specifically references advanced cognitive ability and all that accompanies that capacity, which not all individuals possess.

CHAPTER TWO

Understanding Giftedness (on Its Own Terms)

This chapter gives a closer look at common characteristics, dynamics, and behaviors of gifted children. There are well-documented lists of gifted characteristics, including important factors like a love of learning or an insatiable curiosity. I want to bring us beyond a typical table of contents and share more deeply about what I see to offer a bit of illumination, and perhaps relief, to readers.

Keep in mind that each of these characteristics bring strengths, even when it may be difficult to see. In most cases, the strengths balance out the challenges only with parental kindness, understanding, and nurturing. Complicating matters, one or both parents often share these same challenges or remember experiencing them.

It can be difficult to witness and support what you have not yet resolved within yourself. Throughout this book, there will be ideas to support your own development in service to supporting your child's. While it may not be easy, spending time to reflect and kindheartedly work through these challenges for yourself will help your child's development and fortify their ability to do the same.

Gifted Characteristics

Gifted children, adolescents, teens, and adults can both soar and struggle with facets of a gifted characteristic or dynamic. Here and in subsequent chapters we explore the importance of nurturing these key parts of gifted nature. They can be difficult to discern and extremely challenging for parents and educators to understand. These characteristics and behaviors often serve important developmental and coping purposes, but until we know how to **SEE** and **SUPPORT** this properly, these gifted qualities within ourselves and our children can be misperceived as intentional misbehavior, disrespect, negative, troublesome, and, at worst, pathological.

Intensity

Gifted people wrangle with intensity. It sometimes brings us to intellectual focus, new discovery, and accomplishment, but it can also bring us to our knees emotionally, especially as we experience important human feeling experiences like love, loss, and anger.

As adults, we have had a lifetime of experience with this intensity and we have developed strategies—healthy or not—for quelling or leveraging this energy. But gifted children, adolescents, and teens commonly become swept away by their intensity, sometimes taking others (parents) along for the wild ride, to later feel (again) intensely deep regret, embarrassment, shame, and sometimes a sense of being out of control.

A FEW EXAMPLES OF WHAT WE MIGHT SEE

- ▶ Trouble with transitions, particularly when focused.
- ▶ Trouble with schedule changes.
- ▶ Upset over perceived sibling injustices.
- ▶ Difficulty tolerating game play when losing.
- ▶ Seeming overreaction at ordinary mishaps.

- Deep disappointment when let down by a friend, sibling, or parent.
- Remorse and angry self-statements during or after arguments with parents.

A FEW WAYS WE CAN SUPPORT

- Listen.
- Reflect (see chapter 3).
- Lovingly support your child through outbursts (see chapter 5).
- Normalize—let your child know intensity is part of being human, part of growing up, and especially part of being gifted.
- Advise your child that you have their back, no matter what, and you will get through this together.
- If your child states they wish they had never been born or wish they were dead during or in the aftermath of intensity, do not dismiss these statements. Take them seriously, even for a young child. Seek gifted counseling or psychology services to support your child.

Sensitivity

Gifted people are keenly sensitive. We tend to be sensitive in our emotional (Daniels and Piechowski 2009) empathic, and social experiences, in our nervous and sensory systems, and potentially in other physiological responses in our physical bodies as well (Karpinski, Kinase Kolb, Tetreault, and Borowski 2018).

A FEW EXAMPLES OF WHAT WE MIGHT SEE

- Easily hurt feelings.
- Overly involved in adult/parental issues.
- Finding some school content, world news, and events overwhelming.

- A tendency to wish to help the underdog and the powerless.
- A hatred of human inequities and injustices.
- Spontaneous crying.

A FEW WAYS WE CAN **SUPPORT**

- Sincerely listen and reflect concerns without trying to change your child's mind.
- Shelter your child from your own adult problems.
- Limit or remove access to conventional television news sources (particularly before bedtime and in the car), and work to provide a news source that is less sensational for their access.
- Your child may be concerned about another child at school who is experiencing classmate bullying or has a difficult relationship with a teacher. Do what you can to be a sounding board for your child. With their permission, you may also choose to confidentially advise the school.
- Be available and prepared to answer questions about challenging topics honestly, but carefully, without projecting your own fears.
- Ask: What are those tears saying? (See The Virtues Project in Resources)
- Watch for light, sound, and touch sensitivities and contact a pediatric occupational therapist who understands giftedness for an evaluation.

In my clinical experience, I have discovered that gifted children, adolescents, teens, and adults who do not appear to others to be emotionally, empathically, or socially sensitive are, paradoxically, some of the most sensitive among us. This dynamic leads to a massive misunderstanding of a child's nature as they struggle to cope with overwhelming feelings.

It is a challenge for them to stay grounded, so they often bury their sensitivities, feelings, and experiences.

SEE: You may see these individuals tether themselves to concrete interests and career paths like science, academics, and engineering because there is seemingly less focus in these areas on expression of feelings.

SUPPORT: If instead their sensitivities are acknowledged, celebrated, and nurtured, these types of gifted individuals may still choose this same path to a grounded data-driven career, yet it will be enhanced by an authentic understanding of their tender sensibilities, perhaps leading to great intuitive leaps of discovery and innovation.

SUPPORT: Take inventory in your family on this one and stay open to the possibility that your apparently *least sensitive* family member is perhaps underground, and what looks like uncaring, unfeeling behavior is maybe a brilliant coping camouflage for a sensitive center that could benefit from kind and safe encouragement.

Perfectionism

Gifted perfectionism is a powerful force. It makes us want everything we accomplish or create to be *perfect*. And because we are so naturally skilled at some things, we erroneously believe, especially when we are children, that if we cannot grasp or produce something perfectly in every area of our life and learning, there is something wrong with us.

In one of its loveliest expressions, gifted perfectionism can move us harmoniously into excellence, no matter our age or experience level. Yet, this same quicksilver muse can furnish a self-destructive tendency rooted in self-preservation. We will take ourselves out of the game entirely or, worse, sideline ourselves before even starting the game if we are not sure we can accomplish it with perfection. When we do this as adults it is unfortunate, as we turn away from experiences that might stretch us, or even greatness that might await. But when a child does this it can be devastating, particularly if a pattern of avoidance around ordinary tasks develops.

WHAT WE MIGHT SEE

Avoidance born of perfectionism is a common experience for gifted and twice-exceptional children, teens, and adults, especially if twice-exceptional learning or processing challenges have not been identified and supported.

- Not trying new things.
- Wrenching stress before an important event.
- Unrealistic goals or objectives.
- Exiting opportunities and activities early due to perceived sense of not being skillful.
- Overworked, driven behavior.
- Devastation at perceived or real failure.

HOW WE MIGHT SUPPORT

If your child is avoiding work or completing work but not handing it in, take a closer look at identifying underlying and hidden learning or processing challenges (see the sidebar on page 16).

- Allow children and teens to observe before they try something new. Give them privacy to try something new.
- Check your own perfectionism. Try not to add fuel to the fire of your child's perfectionism.
- Retract any unrealistic expectations you may have for your child or yourself. Because gifted children are asynchronously mature in some ways, at least sometimes, we can erroneously expect too much from them.

- Negotiating exit plans prior to beginning a new activity. For example, if you are enrolling your child in an eight-week fencing program, you agree together on attendance expectations; maybe they are expected to attend five weeks before they can withdraw. However, if you sense the program is socially stressful, emotionally unsafe, or impacting self-esteem, do not hesitate to disenroll your child sooner.

Perceptivity

Gifted individuals notice so much about the environments they live and learn in. We notice patterns and subtle changes to these patterns. We sense those around us, and we sense how those around us might perceive us. Sometimes we can even see cause and effect, or other people's well-concealed agendas or motivations. We perceive and adjust our vocabularies and speech to match those around us.

The great gift of perceptivity can, however, become especially problematic for gifted children when they encounter concealed turmoil in their home or school environment. Children can perceive when something is off, but often can't quite construct a fully accurate understanding of what is actually going on.

I have become a fan of Dr. Stephen Porges's brilliant Polyvagal Theory (Porges 2017), which adds another level of depth and complexity to consider when discussing perceptivity and emotional well-being. His work shows us that as humans, we continually scan our relationships and environment for threat, a process he calls *neuroception*. Our experiences of threat and safety impact our nervous system and subsequent behaviors. Without reliable, safe attunement, and co-regulation between children and their caregivers, children struggle to properly develop self-regulation, which can cycle back as behavioral and other concerns.

Confusing behaviors that can look highly disorganized, dysregulated, and uncharacteristically intense. Or, overall withdrawal.

HOW WE CAN SUPPORT

- Self-reflect on your own well-being. If you experience escalated levels of stress, anxiety, anger, disappointment, frustration, grief, or any other strong human distress, even if it is temporary, or seemingly "well-hidden" from your child, you will need to address and balance this in order for your perceptive gifted child to be able to find their balance. Seek assistance and support if necessary.
- If there is turmoil at home—for example, a quiet and minor, but escalated, parental conflict—let your child know you realize they may be feeling a wave of distress, but that they can let it go. As parents you are figuring something out; that is part of relationships and it is your responsibility, not the child's. Do not involve the child in the conflict.
- Pay attention to turmoil at school. This can come in the form of leadership or educator issues. A perceptive gifted child or teen can sense the distress in the environment, even when unfamiliar with the facts.

Empathic Nature

A characteristic related to gifted sensitivity and perceptivity is gifted empathic nature. In my experience, gifted empathy goes beyond the capacity to understand another's experience by virtue of being human. Gifted young people and adults can actually experience some parts of another's feelings and experiences as their own. However, the translation is often off, impacting the child's emotional field, particularly the ability to regulate anxiety and anger, leading to distressing or troublesome inner experiences and/or behaviors. Once we can understand and work with our empathic nature it is a remarkable ally, but in childhood we need a little guidance.

WHAT WE MIGHT SEE

- Disorganized behavior.
- Uncharacteristic language—sometimes even foul language.
- Escalated anger or anxiety coming seemingly out of nowhere.
- Difficulty calming.
- Confusion.
- Tearfulness or sadness without an obvious cause.

HOW WE MIGHT SUPPORT

A great place to start is by asking your child how they experience you. For example, after returning home from a stressful errand, you might ask, "I was just feeling frustration at the store earlier, could you feel that when I got home just now?" Keep these conversations going and give your child practice in discerning how their frustration feels versus how your frustration feels to them. Help them try to sort out what belongs to them and what belongs to someone else. Do the same exercise with your child after you have cleared or calmed your frustration.

Instead of distracting your child away from difficult feelings, try to sort out with them what is underneath their feelings. When did they begin to feel this way? What was going on then? Where were they? Who were they with? I suggest you wait until strong feelings like anger calm before starting this conversation.

Asynchrony

Asynchrony is often thought of as uneven development in different areas of a gifted child's life experience (Silverman 1992, 1993, 1997, 2013a, 2013b, [in press]; Neville, Piechowski, et al. 2013) and can manifest in a variety of ways such as twice-exceptionality, when giftedness is accompanied with a learning, processing, emotional, or physical challenge, or other exceptionality like autism. This can be especially perplexing for a child who is highly gifted and twice-exceptional. Asynchrony can also be present as it relates to a child's maturity levels and coping strategies in different areas of their lives.

Asynchrony can be exhausting for our children to manage alone without support. These contrary dynamics, in my experience, often underpin frustration and anger, but parents and educators can miss this in children at first. Helping your child by working to understand their asynchronies and supporting them is key to their well-being, your relationship, and sometimes family harmony. Because it is related to development, you can expect these asynchronies to somewhat shift and change as your child grows, especially if there is effective intervention for the learning, sensory, processing, or other challenge.

WHAT WE MIGHT SEE

- ► Children capable of discussing something intellectual with an adult mentor, but sob like a toddler over an unexpected schedule change or small disappointment.
- ► A young gifted child struggling to capture their advanced thoughts and ideas in writing or drawing foiled by their young fine motor skills, not being able to keep up.
- ► A profoundly gifted child who can't read well (or at all) due to dyslexia.

► Become as fluent as you can in asynchrony in general and begin to track and address your child's differences from this higher perspective, knowing that things will continue to change.

► When your child is frustrated or angry, do some detective work. Watch for patterns, signs, indications of what is under frustration, and support your child's development in this area by arranging for evaluations to determine twice-exceptionality (see page 20) or other supports you can put in place.

Fairness and Sense of Justice

Gifted individuals of all ages have a sharp and innate sense of what seems fair and just, and conversely, what seems unfair and unjust.

WHAT WE MIGHT SEE

► You will see gifted children, adolescents, teens, and adults abandon an entire relationship, commitment, or ideological concept if they encounter a shred of injustice, sometimes refusing to reengage even in the spirit of reconciliation, growth, or learning.

► Further compounding this dynamic and frustrating parents is when young gifted children, due to their age, intensity, and perfectionism, will sometimes not be able to see, in the moment, these same unjust power discrepancies or differentials that trouble them within their own actions, particularly toward younger siblings.

► Gifted young people may see and feel themselves as ineffective or incapable of righting massive injustices they see in the world.

- Support your child's interest to become involved in change movements and projects.
- Research together the stories of ordinary people who impacted change.
- Work to embody fairness and justice in your own home, interactions, and choices.
- Discuss the up-and-down nature of human relationships and friendships with your child when they have been disappointed with a friend (see chapter 6).
- Show kindness to your young gifted child who may behave unjustly toward younger siblings. They have awareness of this asynchrony or discrepancy, and most likely are embarrassed by it. After the storm has passed, talk through with them what is at the heart of their distress. Plan together to address valid, current complaints and how to address future issues (see chapter 3).

Creativity and Well-being

Gifted individuals are creative in different ways. Yet creativity can become sidetracked or stunted through formal education (Robinson and Aronica, 2015), family disapproval or differences, or a child's willingness to conceal part of who they are to fit in.

Gifted creativity certainly lives through creative expression and the arts, but it can go far beyond this into our interests, self-expression, and life path. Having sovereignty in your creative expression as a human, especially when you are young, underscores, supports and furthers the potential in everything else you will learn and explore intellectually.

Sadly, in my experience, sometimes a gifted child, adolescent, or teen does not have a way to fully express who they are in the moment because they believe it conflicts with the way their family or peers see things. If we can't begin to express and be accepted for our true self when we are young, we can get off course in some tragic ways.

WHAT WE MIGHT SEE

- Frustration in art class with a teaching focus on product versus process.
- Inaccurately comparing their creative expression with a classmate who has a different style, approach, and expression. This is especially true for gifted children who have not yet fully developed their fine motor skill, when comparing themselves to someone who draws realistically.
- Frustration or boredom in music classes that only focus on repetition, mastering pieces, and voice and instrument management versus experimentation, composition, and improvisation.
- Hiding sense of style or interest in good design from family because it may not be taken seriously or because it may be rejected or deemed frivolous.

WAYS TO SUPPORT

- Let your gifted child know they are free to be themselves in your home and in your family. Free them from misaligned social expectations and help them find a way to be true to themself while navigating these often rigid parameters. Offer this support outside the home as well, although there may be times when the two of you will have to brainstorm to plan ahead and adjust. For example, fielding questions from grandparents about taking a gap year to study something alternative.

- Choose activities and instructors carefully. Listen to your child's input about their teachers and experiences and adjust accordingly.
- Sometimes it takes exaggerated creative endeavor to more fully unlock where your sense of self lives. It may actually be closer to where parents, peers, and society live as well, however this destination should be reached organically through self-expression and exploration in a supportive, accepting environment.

A Complicated Relationship with Humanity

In my experience, gifted children, adolescents, teens, and adults tend to have a love-hate relationship with humanity. They want to help alleviate human suffering and contribute to solving large-scale humanitarian problems, while they simultaneously feel repulsed witnessing individual or collective complacency, injustice, malevolence, or foolishness. This conflict exists within themselves as well as they reconcile their own behaviors, realizing that they are human, and perhaps have even contributed to the same problems that repulse them.

WHAT WE MIGHT SEE

- Sadness, anxiety, existential depression
- Anger with self
- Feeling powerless

WAYS WE MIGHT SUPPORT

The best balm for this experience is getting in touch with your own conflicts in this area. Then, set aside a neutral and loving time to begin an ongoing conversation with your child.

Existential Dilemma

Most humans think about their existence and contemplate human existential dilemmas arising from questions like: *What is the meaning of life? What is the meaning of my life? Even if I am loved and a valued part of a family or community, why do I still feel alone?* Gifted children and adolescents are not different, but they begin to think about these matters of existence deeply when they are young and these thoughts can feel overwhelming because they do not have adult life experience (another example of asynchrony). It is important to start this conversation with your child when you have inklings that they are working through something existential.

WHAT WE MIGHT SEE

You may know it is time to address existential concerns through their existential questions or comments, appearances of general sadness or fear, or through extended withdrawal or silence. You may also see signs within their responses to learning about difficult news like a natural, accidental, or suicidal death.

WAYS WE MIGHT SUPPORT

▸ Become expert at reading these silences and expressions.
▸ Create an agreement with your child to be together, even if it is just sitting together when these moments happen for your child.
▸ Be supportive through listening and reflecting.
▸ Do not dismiss these concerns.
▸ If there is something that helps you through this part of being human, like poetry or a biography, share this with your child.
▸ Seek gifted counseling support.

Love of Learning, Critical Thinking, and Problem Solving

It is crucial to give gifted young people room to independently and collectively think, create, and problem-solve beyond the confines of school.

WHAT WE MIGHT SEE

Deep research, questioning, and seeking experience in unusual topics.

HOW WE MIGHT SUPPORT

- Stay open to what your child wishes to explore and support these impulses to see where they lead.
- Your child may stay with some things for awhile but move on quickly from others. Do not be surprised or frustrated when this happens.
- Trust your child's sense of when it is time to move on.
- Resist overpowering, overshadowing, or overwhelming your child with your own knowledge in the area.
- If you can, set up your home and learning environments to be resourceful places where it is okay to make mistakes and there is at least one area where it is okay to create or leave projects (messes) in progress while doing so.
- Help your child by viewing "failed" explorations as a crucial part of the learning, critical thinking, and problem-solving processes. There are many examples of innovation birthed from failure. Learn more about the greatest inventors and entrepreneurs and share what you find at the dinner table. Much human innovation was born from failure.
- If your child's interests require instruction or lessons that are expensive, and you are concerned they will drop out before completion, talk about this with your child beforehand to map out a reasonable agreement.

Keen Sense of Humor

Gifted people tend to have magnificent senses of humor. It ties closely to their relationship to humanity as well as their perceptivity and empathic capacity. However, it is sometimes not appreciated by the classroom teacher, school administration, classmates, or family members who find observations off-putting or hitting too close to home.

WHAT WE MIGHT SEE

▶ Extroverted children can have trouble putting the mic down, even when they have lost their audience.

▶ Introverted children may not speak up in a public setting, like school, losing the opportunity to have their comedic talent recognized.

▶ As parents, teachers, and counselors, we can help both become more self-aware and skillful.

HOW WE MIGHT SUPPORT

▶ Kindheartedly help your child become more self-aware of their tendencies to overwhelm others or remain unseen. Ask them how they would like it to be. Brainstorm together what might help. Let your child know this is part of being human, part of growing up, and part of being gifted. It's okay and you will get through this together.

▶ Sometimes, humans use humor to offset the pain of being human. It can be important to spot-check or scan for what is under the surface of your child's humor, especially if it tends to circle around a particular topic.

▶ It is useful to direct your child away from sarcasm and toward a more evolved expression of humor—this will also help your child's self-esteem and humor development. If you are sarcastic, try to move yourself toward a different, less negative expression of humor.

Dabrowski's Theory of Positive Disintegration

Kazimierz Dabrowski (1902–1980) was a Polish psychiatrist and psychologist. He worked on a theory of personality development called the Theory of Positive Disintegration (TPD) that outlined the components of a process for individuals to reach a personality ideal. When introduced to this theory the greater gifted community became particularly interested in, and remains focused on, the part of the theory that translates as *overexcitability* or *overexcitabilities* (Piechowski 1979; Daniels and Piechowski 2009; Piechowski 2014; Rivero 2010, 2010).

The five areas of overexcitability were seen by Dabrowski as indicators of an individual's potential to develop. Some or all of these overexcitabilities are frequently seen in the makeup of gifted children, adolescents, teens, and adults. Manifestations of overexcitabilities can be seen as deficits, strengths, or both, depending on the lens of the viewer.

In my practice, I present these concepts in a general sense, and as strengths, and say that they represent an individual's developmental potential. Some people have all five, some people have fewer—whatever you have is perfect. Learning about these overexcitabilities will help you learn more about your child's particular traits and how you can nurture these strengths and navigate accompanying challenges.

Psychomotor Overexcitability

People with this overexcitability need to move, whether it be through athletics, dance, or in simple gestures like continued drumming on the table, pacing, or with a constantly moving foot when seated. They often talk quickly as well.

These children need to have access to regular movement. Walking down the street with family, you may find them up on walls, swinging from a low tree branch, and running ahead and back frequently. Find and plan ways to support your child through movement.

Imaginational Overexcitability

People with this overexcitability have great capacity to imagine, so can be wonderful problem-solvers, inventors, storytellers, and screenwriters. Theirs is an ongoing approach to life where their imagination is in near full swing, appearing frequently to daydream.

It can be helpful for these children to have family support to explore imaginatively. Regularly let your child know they have a wonderful imagination, and ask if there is anything they need from you to support this. Some children wish to have help acting out scenes. Some wish to learn filmmaking by borrowing an old device with a camera. Some wish to have a designated table or space to store materials, create, and invent. Some need more access to nature.

Emotional Overexcitability

These individuals feel their feelings deeply. They embody the highs and lows of human emotional experience, which can be especially challenging and overwhelming when young. They can also feel the feelings of others and the joy and pain of the world deeply. These are the children who can experience overwhelm when encountering life circumstances such as observing families experiencing homelessness, attending a class lesson on genocide, or visiting an animal shelter.

Talk regularly with children about this as you encounter the world with them. Help them debrief difficult experiences. Help them prepare for potentially difficult experiences—for example, entering a space that might feel overwhelming, like a big commercial box store. Once you leave the store, help them debrief what it was like to be inside and tend to anything they may need to settle back in.

Intellectual Overexcitability

These individuals are continually interested in engaging and understanding the world beyond the scope of typical school curriculum. They are constantly seeking, curious to learn and understand more.

Often it seems perplexing to parents as their child shifts completely away from a deep exploration into the next area of interest. I encourage you to follow and support your child's interests closely, but do not get too attached right away as this interest may only be temporary, sometimes serving to scaffold the next pursuit, sometimes not.

Sensual Overexcitability

Sensual overexcitability translates to a love of the sensual parts of the human experience, specifically where we might find beauty: nature, music, design, art, architecture, poetry, and sensual pleasures like food.

These are generally easy to spot as you track your child's lead, but I often find a child's sensual overexcitability is not shared in the same way or at all by their parents, who have different sensibilities. Quite common are children who have a strong sense of beautiful design but this is unimportant to their parents, who do not necessarily give the same importance to clothing, home, or other design. Depending on your sensibilities, you may need to flex a bit to support your child in this area. Do not shrug off sensual overexcitability, which can erroneously seem superficial.

With the intention of providing a fuller picture of Dabrowski's work I offer you a thumbnail sketch of TPD beyond the overexcitabilities to contemplate as you support the gifted young people you parent and serve.

Dabrowski proposed that in order to develop our personalities into our highest ideal, it is necessary to break down or disintegrate less evolved personality structures and the accompanying ways of thinking and behaving. This process requires internal as well as external tension to create the conditions to move ahead in our development. In other words, it is the difficulties of our inner and outer lives that provide the tension required to evolve. Dabrowski saw this tension at the heart of things like anxiety and depression, which he felt were not maladies to pathologize, but rather indicators of the tension that emerges as we attempt to navigate and evolve within a world full of human trauma, suffering, pain, detrimental power differentials, and foolishness.

Dabrowski outlined several factors that work within us and underscore this developmental process: our nature (or genetics), our nurture (or environment), and our inner resource and drive, which he called our third factor. Some of these processes can happen spontaneously, others are cultivated through awarenesses. Some development may occur more quickly, other development much more slowly. The positive disintegration process will repeat as new development is approached and attempted, and there may be long stretches of time between new phases of development (Dabrowski 1964; Daniels and Piechowski 2009; Mendaglio 2008; Silverman 1993).

I encourage you to look more deeply into this work. By doing so, you can help support the development process, which can be rough. It is possible to access some of Dabrowski's translated work in hardcopy and electronic formats thanks to the diligence of some of his former students who still, along with others, tend the flame of his work.

INTENSITY IS A GIFT; NURTURE IT

If you want your gifted child to thrive, then you must stay open to the possibility that many of their intense, nonconforming behaviors can lead to wonderful places when understood and nurtured instead of extinguished. For example, we can fortify an intense child's capacity to speak up in a way that can be received well by others instead of quieting them in the name of polite behavior. You do your child no favors by trying to "cure" the behaviors that arise from their giftedness for the sake of the status quo.

This means you may need to reframe your relationship with extended family that do not understand your child or disagree with your parenting. You may also need to redefine your relationship to authority, such as in educational and health-care systems, as you determine what is in your child's best interests to learn, live, and survive healthily.

There is certainly a time and place for interventions, but if they grossly subdue or destroy a bright child's fire or developmental tension in the process, the cost may outweigh the benefit for the child, and for us all.

As we, alongside our children, watch the breakdown of our environment and our educational, economic, social, health-care, and political systems and structures, why would we want to subdue our brilliant children's intensity or wild creativity? Because it is off-putting, inconvenient, noncompliant, off-center, quirky, or truth-telling?

Why aren't we collectively *listening* to what is underneath the anxiety of children, and in this context, perceptive gifted children?

Many gifted young people may not be able to live easily within the parameters of our social institutions and contracts, but that does not necessarily mean they are wrong, misdirected, or misbehaved. What cost do we pay when we force our brightest children into a path that leaves little space for their nonconforming goodwill and massively creative and intellectual impulses?

Why do we tend to quell these anxious behaviors through a variety of interventions aimed at changing their perspective versus finding calm by intelligently challenging the status quo? Dabrowski had a term for this tragedy; he called it *positive maladjustment,* where we (mal)adapt to live in a world that is not what it could or should be (Dabrowski, Piechowski et al. 1970; Mayer, Perkins, et al. 2001; Piechowski; 2014).

It is monumental work to be a parent, educator, or counselor and stand behind and for these bright, creative children.

CHAPTER THREE

Parenting Within a Gifted Family

Parenting gifted children is, of course, in many ways similar to parenting any child. Your focus is to provide a safe, nurturing home for your child to find security, love, and support that they can count on and return to as they develop, grow, and experience the world outside the family nest. But sometimes as a parent of a gifted child you may feel embarrassed about your parenting because you have tried traditional parenting approaches that simply do not work for you or your child. That's completely understandable.

Together we'll look at some strategies that are more likely to help you create harmony within your family. Parenting within a gifted family is its own universe, requiring dedicated self-reflection, superhuman agility, and perseverance built upon a foundation of love, relationship, and respect.

Healthy Parents, Healthy Children

In my experience, gifted children tend to have parents who have gifted characteristics or are gifted, even if this has not been identified formally nor recognized informally. So if you're reading this book because your child has been identified as gifted, you and your partner may be gifted, too.

Understandably, this revelation can come with mixed emotional experiences, some very challenging: grief for lost time or potential; anger over feeling misunderstood or unsupported as a child; denial, in that it is not you, but the child's other parent's genetics that solely accounts for the giftedness (possible, but unlikely); deep sadness for extended family who were not seen as gifted and chose less healthy coping strategies; and a late awakening to unowned or disowned parts of yourself.

Be kind to yourself. Acknowledge that you are the perfect parent for your child as a result. Children often help us see exactly what we need to see in ourselves. However, it is easy to misinterpret the message and project our own challenges or distress onto the child's behavior instead of doing the harder work of looking inward.

Even if you have not been formally identified as gifted, it is imperative to find a good counselor who understands giftedness and resolve any issues you may have that affect your child. Otherwise, the impact of this family legacy will interfere with your child's development and continue down through the generations of your family tree.

If you are identified as gifted, the single most important thing you can do to help your gifted child to thrive is to self-reflect. You need to become clear on where you may need support for yourself as a gifted adult. Ask yourself the following questions:

- Are you challenged by your own intensity or perfectionism?
- Do you ignore, override, or overtax your perceptivity or sensitivity, or numb it through work, overachievement, addiction, or self-medication?
- Do you avoid engaging with your feelings or find you are overwhelmed by them?
- Do you suspect you have an unrecognized twice-exceptionality?
- Are you feeling "checked out" with life in general?

If this sounds like you, don't despair. Understand that by addressing these concerns you will resolve issues within yourself and also gain greater insight into how best to parent your gifted child. If you are challenged in these or other ways, take this time now to address these concerns.

Get on the Same Parenting Page

Couples therapists Harville Hendrix and Helen LaKelly Hunt tell us that partners are drawn together on some level to work through what they each could not work out as children with their own parents and family (Hendrix and Hunt 2019). This is a beautiful benefit of partnering, but, unless it is honored and tended to, it can eventually move partners apart. Without awareness, in my experience, it can also create a conflicted and lopsided parenting approach that can detrimentally impact a child's relationship with their parents as well as their social-emotional development. When you throw gifted family intensity, perfectionism, and sensitivity into this mix, the family system can become deeply stressed.

It is critical that parents take time to come together and examine their childhoods and the ways they were parented, then begin a discussion about what worked for them (or not), and how they wish to parent their own children. If parents are separated, divorced, or across two homes, I still recommend trying to do this, if it is possible. You may be surprised to learn that sometimes parents who seem to be more permissive had more authoritarian or disciplinarian parents, and parents who had hands-off or permissive parents wish to parent with a sterner approach. These same impulses can appear in who they have chosen as a partner as well.

It is possible to find a parenting approach that feels authentic and in sync with your partner, but this takes continued communication and an agreement that you will do this together and share consensus in decision-making. If you disagree about some component of your parenting, have an understanding and a plan to try to work together and not undermine each other, no matter what. Your child will feel this cohesion and thrive within it. Your child will also feel if there is disharmony and will struggle deeply.

Opposing Natures, Opposing Needs

As if there were not enough complexity and paradox in gifted families, I also notice that gifted families are composed of parents, partners, children, and siblings who are frequently opposite in nature and require diametrically opposed support—for example, introverts who live with extroverts, sensory-seeking individuals who live with sensory-avoidant individuals, and visual-spatial people who live with auditory-sequential people.

It is important that each member of the family have what they need to live well, recharge, and engage. A helpful course of action is to begin to raise awareness of each person's different needs by talking about this as a family. You can plan together how you will communicate what everyone needs, how they want those needs met, and what to do when needs are not being met.

Here are some examples of the pitfalls facing families in this area:

- The parents are sensory-avoidant but the children are sensory-seeking, wishing to be frequently held, snuggled, or wrestled with. When parents need a break, it needs to be communicated in a way so the child does not feel rejected or wrong. If your child is sensory-seeking or sensory-avoidant, it can help them to be evaluated by and work with a skilled pediatric occupational therapist.

- On a family camping trip or vacation, an introverted child wishes to remain back to read a book rather than hike or sightsee. Forcing the child to come along sets the stage for a dismal day. Leaving the child behind creates a safety dilemma. Instead, families can talk about this in advance, securing a child's input and buy-in, and coordinating a meaningful plan to furnish the child with dedicated down time during the family trip for reading and relaxing.

- Introverted parents not knowing how to connect with other parents to plan or host get-togethers for their extroverted child. If this is you, are not alone. Start simply. Find out who your child wants to meet with and collect parent contact information—this may be the hardest step as you may have to really push yourself to track this down. (In chapter 6, we will discuss putting together social plans for your child.)

- Perfectionistic visual-spatial children who procrastinate with their schoolwork with perfectionistic auditory-sequential, detail-oriented, and time-organized parents. This dynamic ruins many a Sunday night for gifted families as children rush to complete their work at the last minute, perhaps requiring parental help to track down materials. Parents feel frustrated because this could have been accomplished in a more organized way during the week. I will give you guidance on working through procrastination in the next chapter.

▶ In comparing younger siblings to older gifted siblings, parents will sometimes erroneously believe their younger children are not gifted because they have different natures, expressions, habits, and behaviors than their older child/ren.

FAMILY, A HOUSE OF MIRRORS OF SHADOW AND LIGHT

The term shadow comes from Carl Jung's work on archetypes (Jung, 1979). Our shadow is often mostly unknown to us and can be a disruptive force in our lives, as we dislike the shadow aspects we may hold or may not be aware of. We become uncomfortable when we sense or see our shadow aspects in other people. This is true even when we are unaware of these aspects within ourselves. Our light aspects, on the other hand, tend to be the parts of ourselves we like. Parts of both of these aspects can be in our conscious awareness and, by virtue of being human, we have the potential to access a wide range of human shadow and light. As a result, this can feel unsettling.

When we encounter someone we are drawn to, they often hold a part of our light, sometimes even a part we have not yet ignited or become aware of within ourselves. It usually feels enlivening to be with people who reflect or bring out our light. Think of how you feel with certain people who bring out the best in you.

When we encounter someone who we are triggered or repulsed by, they often hold a part of our shadow, sometimes even a part we have not yet acknowledged, or a part that we have disowned because it is difficult to see or admit we have it within ourselves. It is usually challenging to be around or witness the actions of people who remind us, even unconsciously, of our shadow. You have likely encountered people who rubbed you the wrong way even if you couldn't put your finger on exactly why.

Within our family, like any community of humans, we can see aspects of ourselves. This can be delightful when these aspects hold our light, and painful when these aspects hold our shadow. This is partly why parents become so upset with their children as what they are witnessing in the child is something they also struggle with.

A helpful exercise to try to get to the bottom of your shadow aspects to begin to heal them is to ask yourself, when you are triggered by someone: **What about this person, or this aspect, is about me too?** *Try to stay open to the answers and possibilities that may arise.*

Once we can see and acknowledge our shadow aspects, we can begin to befriend these parts of ourselves that are calling for our attention. Sometimes our shadow aspects develop as a coping response from childhood that we no longer need. Sometimes our shadow aspects develop through patterns or personalities from our family of origin that were never really who we were anyway, and it is a relief to acknowledge and release them, freeing ourselves and often our children as well from this distress.

Gifted Intensity and Anger in the Family Tree

As we have discussed, gifted people are more intense in many areas of their lives, including their emotional lives, which can translate to anger, outbursts, and high tension in gifted homes.

As humans, we tend to become angriest with those we feel safest with. When your child lets their anger roar with you, it is because they feel safe with you—it is the highest compliment they can pay you (Hegberg 2002). This is not the case if parents are mean-spirited, narcissistic, addicted, or punitive; children from these families will find other outlets, like school, or sometimes self-injury for their anger. If this is happening for your child, I advise you to seek kindhearted professional assistance to untangle this as soon as possible.

If the safest place for you to release your anger is with your child, I also suggest you seek support to sort this out in order to free your parent-child relationship, and your child's well-being, from the tyranny of this dynamic. Conversely, if you keep in all of your anger, allowing it to only simmer into passive aggression or inner turmoil, I suggest, without judgment, that you seek support to free yourself from the oppression of this perfectionism. This may be difficult for you to hear, but often helping yourself by cultivating healthy behavior is the best way to help your children.

Interestingly, anger is usually not a primary emotion. Often there is some other feeling or a constellation of feelings beneath the surface of anger. What is underneath our anger varies between circumstances, settings, and with different people.

In my experience, one of the best first steps in helping a child eventually understand their anger and gain clarity about their needs is to independently work to discover what lives under your own anger. You want to begin by looking at your own anger before you try to help your child, otherwise this strategy will not work. Then, in the calm, a day or so after an angry outburst, begin to gently discuss with your child, in a nonjudgmental or defensive way, what is possibly underneath their anger as well. Let them know this can happen for you, too. This may illuminate for both of you concerning experiences and feelings—important information that you will want to continue to discuss and address, perhaps professionally, as you support their development. If you are not sure how to start this conversation, begin with reflection, which we will discuss later in this chapter.

For perfectionistic gifted children, who hold it all together at school, enduring and repressing the endless small injustices and slow or meaningless learning, you may notice a release or deluge of seemingly unrelated anger at the end of the school day directed at you or, often, a sibling.

Help your child make the connection here and give them a sounding board to talk frankly about hardships at school. Let them know you support them, help them problem-solve and develop awareness so they can begin to self-advocate while you perhaps reevaluate school fit. Again, start with reflection to get this conversation underway.

If one or several parts of a child's family tree has anger concerns, an exceptionally angry child may actually, subconsciously, be trying to break the family pattern, by calling attention to it. If individuals within the family do not address, nor succeed in shifting, this entrenched pattern, like other family patterns it can travel with the family tree to the next generation (Bowen 1966, 2004). Reframing and following your child's noble lead provides you with an opportunity to help break unhelpful patterns that maybe once served your family but no longer do. Find a counselor who truly understands giftedness, intensity, and family systems, and who can go far beyond the strategies of cognitive and behavioral modification for your *angry* gifted child.

Anger and outbursts are seen as inappropriate, yet they hold so much important information that we need to know. I suggest parents reframe these instances as valuable. Your child is trying to tell you something important. And don't worry, we will go over the best ways to handle these moments in the next chapter.

Gifted People Who Cope by Withdrawing

Children who are introverted or tend to be more inward will often withdraw rather than have an outburst (although they can have outbursts too). Instead, those challenging feelings build and embed within your child, causing much internal distress.

For parents of a gifted child who is more inward and perfectionistic, it can be difficult to discern when something is troubling them and easy to miss opportunities to intervene when they are in distress or crisis. Teachers of these children, unless they know what to look for, often advise parents that their child is a model student because, essentially, they do not misbehave or challenge classroom management practices.

If your child fits this description, it is optimal to start an ongoing conversation with them about their nature, which is fine but needs to find a way to self-express, hopefully leading to self-advocacy.

Withdrawal can be a form of avoidance, so twice- and multi-exceptional kids are especially at risk for developing this coping strategy. Once locked in, this coping mechanism is difficult to unknot. You might see a twice-exceptional child leave a classroom when content is too challenging, or they might distract away or change the subject of conversation; both are immediate coping strategies to handle not knowing, but in the long term, avoidance at this level will backfire. If you are someone who withdraws or tends to avoid particularly as a coping strategy, you and your child will both benefit if you begin this same dialogue within yourself so you can properly self-express and advocate.

How Empathy Hurts

Any emotion can dissipate at some level when we name it, to ourselves or one another. In my experience as a clinician, I see when a parent is not able to acknowledge or express their own emotions, even to themselves; perceptive, empathic, gifted children can pick up this unacknowledged feeling under the surface and run it as their own. This happens frequently in gifted families and in the classroom setting.

From my perspective, what makes this phenomenon even harder to untangle is that what one person experiences as one emotion, another person most likely will experience as another. For example, if a parent is feeling resentful toward the other parent, but not expressing it, this resentment may show up in their gifted child as sadness, anxiety, or even anger, seemingly unrelated to another cause in the moments before the gifted child became dysregulated.

You have the power to help your child with this by naming your feelings, at least to yourself. Pay close attention to what happens within you as you begin to acknowledge your feelings. Pay close attention to what happens for your child as you begin to acknowledge your feelings.

Mature Discussions

Gifted children often begin to think about matters related to serious topics like death, war, poverty, racism, spirituality, addiction, environmental sustainability, privilege, and existential concerns at an earlier age. Asking parents questions about these topics can leave parents wondering how to respond.

It is okay to let your child know you need some time to collect your thoughts before you respond. It is also okay to advise, in some cases, that you have ideas or answers for them, but may need to wait until they are older to discuss fully.

It can be helpful to strike a balance between giving your child access to appropriate factual information in these areas, like researching the human life span and cycle to discuss death, while simultaneously limiting access to potentially overwhelming sources of information, like nightly news conflict coverage when discussing war.

Sometimes, turning to topical children's literature—fiction, nonfiction, and biography—and reading together can give your child time, space, and access to you to discuss and sort out these matters in a fairly contained but meaningful way. Field trips and visits to historical places, museums, and exhibitions, with a long stretch of preparatory conversation beforehand and debriefing afterward, can be helpful as well.

The benefits of maturity at a younger age include early interests in civics, philosophy, science, equity, justice, and virtue, among other human endeavors. Additionally, these mature topics may spark burgeoning creativity and imagination as children look for ways to resolve human pain and suffering. One of the primary risks of this kind of maturity at a younger age is not having the life experience to negotiate the strong emotion that can accompany this thinking. Children may also feel powerless to help ease the pain of humanity.

Honesty

We each get to decide our relationship to truth-telling. For some, a commitment to truth-telling happens at a younger age, for others when older, and for some, this does not occur at all. Within a personal policy of truth, there are further complications—for example, telling a lie to spare someone pain.

It is developmentally appropriate for children to explore lying as they navigate personal power and moral development milestones. Gifted children, like most children and adults, would prefer not to be deceptive in this way, but sometimes they see no other option when they are trying to accomplish something under their own agency and know their parents may say no—or when they wish to avoid something, when they have forgotten to take care of something, or when their perfectionism gets in the way of the truth, because they want to be perceived as good and perfect.

> *Children, gifted or not, lie rather than face their parents' wrath and severe consequences when their parents are perfectionistic, tend to overreact, or are controlling. These children, like all children, need assistance, safety, and grace to step off this precarious place easefully and into their own policy around their relationship to the truth.*

Getting to Truth-Telling

Parents often find great discomfort and frustration when their children lie to them. It can be helpful to remind yourself that this is part of human development, and it is possible to shift this dynamic between you and your child. I have developed a straightforward way to assist parents and children to change this tendency.

① First, it is helpful to remember that on some level, gifted and twice- or multi-exceptional children, adolescents, teens, and adults tend to hide part of themselves from different parts of their educational, work, and social landscapes in order to fit in better. This is essentially a way they are not living in their truth. So, a less important fib about brushing their teeth to avoid parental disapproval is not that much more of an extension.

② Next, it is vital you help your child see that figuring out fibbing is part of growing up, part of being human, and part of being gifted when you are often a few or many steps ahead of other people. Explain that when they are ready to commit to truth-telling, you will be there to help them get through it together, but you will wait until they are ready to change this dynamic.

③ You will also need to become pristine in your relationship to the truth in order to be credible in this process with your child. You cannot expect your child to make a change that you have not made yourself. So, no more small white lies to bow out of a social commitment or to get off the phone. If you want honesty to be the policy you need to lead by example. If you are living within a larger lie—for example, not being true to yourself or struggling with alcoholism or another addiction— I advise, without judgment, you seek support to sort this out. Your child will not be able to easily break free from dishonesty until you can.

④ You will need to be ready to hear the truth from your child; sometimes, this can be difficult to hear, especially if your child is pointing out something that you may be unwilling to see within your family or yourself.

⑤ When your child is ready to move away from fibbing, you will need to have a private conversation about it. At my office this is how that discussion and agreement goes:

- ▸ If your child promises to tell the truth, whether in the moment or after the fact, you promise to not overreact, ever.
- ▸ Instead, you promise to acknowledge the courage it took for your child to be honest and you promise to help them sort the issue out, especially your part of the equation.
- ▸ If the fib involves something scary or safety-related, explain that you reserve the right to step away to collect yourself. Honor your promise not to overreact but emphasize this does not mean there is not a consequence for the child at some point.
- ▸ Children also promise to let you know when they feel like lying. Or, after a fib, they commit to come back to you to come clean. Decide on simple phrases to convey this, for example: *I feel like lying to you right now,* or *Yesterday, I fibbed and I want to tell you about it.* Again, it is critical that you do not overreact as they take this step. Instead, acknowledge their courage and honesty and talk it through together.
- ▸ Work to understand your part in the child's decision to lie, which might include demanding a certain behavior or response from a child, the child's past experience with your overreaction, or your own perfectionism.
- ▸ Allow your child to work on this privately with you and their other parent. Telling siblings or extended family may be embarrassing for your child.

Working with Perfectionism

As we discussed in chapter 2, perfectionism helps us move toward excellence, but it can also be a debilitating force for gifted children, teens, and adults.

Perfectionism will most likely be an ongoing conversation within your family. You cannot ask a gifted child to just do away with problematic perfectionism. But you can support them to lessen the devastation it can cause. Here are some of my ideas and strategies:

Create a Culture of Mistake-Making Within Your Family

This will help normalize and offset the harsher side of perfectionism. Let your child see and hear about the ordinary mistakes you make. You do this simply by saying out loud, kindheartedly to yourself or others, your own ordinary mistakes. Do this in real time, or shortly after the fact, with your children or the children you teach or counsel. When you have made a mistake in your parenting, by doing something like overreacting or making a poor decision, own this and give your child a genuine apology. List the ways you messed up and provide details, thereby showing your children how to do this part of life honestly, kindly, and well.

Perfectionism Isn't Perfect

Celebrate mistakes as opportunities to learn. Research and talk about discoveries and innovation and accomplishment that could not have happened without mistakes. Ask family friends to describe how a mistake brought them into success. Talk about the flaws that can be found in the idea that everything has to be perfect. I suggest you have these conversations casually and not right after a perfectionistic episode.

Learning to Set Realistic Goals

This is a tough one, especially if you are a goal-setter and your child is not interested. You see the benefit, but they do not—particularly if the goal is something that you desire versus something they desire.

Your best shot is in a moment of neutral calm—maybe at breakfast. Let your child know it is part of your job to help them learn about goal-setting at some point, and that you understand this may not be something they are interested in doing.

Next, pay close attention to what they desire for themselves. It might be something they wish to master, learn about, or wish to obtain or purchase. Later, reflect for your child that you heard their desire earlier and you are willing to help them figure out next steps. Either way, you plan to sit down together to map out ideas and a route to accomplishing this goal. In this conversation, talk honestly and directly about what might get in the way of accomplishing this goal, and what your child wants to do to minimize that possibility.

It can be helpful to physically draw out plans and goals. You can use a calendar just for this purpose too, to measure out the timing.

I deeply caution you to not force your child to go through this process. If you try and it is not successful, let your child know that you can return to this for another reason, at another time, and keep your eyes open for other opportunities.

Process over Outcomes

When your child is trying to accomplish something—anything, great or small—and is struggling, reflect what you see. Use language that acknowledges their efforts, not the outcome. For example, when your child is trying to open a jar but can't, say, *"Charlie, you really tried to open that jar."* This turns what your child might perceive as a failure into more of a mastery experience, honoring the effort and process. Do this all the time, every time you see your child try. Resist the urge to complete the task for your child. This will help your child's development of self-efficacy and strengthen the intrinsic motivation we will discuss further in chapter 5.

Additionally, do not swoop in to accomplish the task for your child, even if it would save time. Allow them to try, and acknowledge this. If your child needs your help, let them ask you directly and then acknowledge that effort: *"Thanks, Charlie, for asking for what you need."* I suggest you use that phrase any time a child asks for what they need. It helps them feel their sense of agency and develop self-advocacy skills, further discussed in chapter 7.

Let Children Talk About Their Work Without Interpreting or Evaluating

When a young child shows us their art, as adults, we can often go right to interpreting what we see. This is not a helpful practice for any child, but especially for gifted children. When a child presents us with their work—art, written, or otherwise—ask them to tell us about it. Ask reflective questions like:

Tell me about what you have created.

How did you decide to choose or approach this topic?

Tell me how you decided to use these colors?

What part of this work surprised you?

What part of this work was most difficult for you? What did you do to overcome that?

Listen closely and reflect back what you hear, word for word, if possible. These exchanges will deepen your relationship with your child, as well as fortify their sense of themselves and their worth. Reflection at this level also provides a bit of relief from perfectionism and the detrimental impact of extrinsic motivation, which we will discuss further in chapter 5.

TRIANGULATION

Triangulation (Bowen 1966, 2004) is an unhealthy psychological and communication dynamic that can happen in families. Families with parents who have a less differentiated sense of self (or who they are in relationship) are especially vulnerable to creating this dynamic within the family. Essentially what occurs is that two family members align and exclude or scapegoat a third, who may play a tension-relieving role for the family system. For example, if there is tension between parents, the child's needs may become the focus of one or both parents to take the heat off or reinvigorate the parent relationship, but in the end this can create more distress for everyone. There can be multiple triangulations within a family system.

The Karpman Drama Triangle (Karpman 2014, 2019) is a concept evident when there is high conflict, drama, and other factors, like addiction, within a family. Each point of the triangle is given a role of victim, rescuer, or persecutor, and family members revolve around these three positions. Generally, one person feels victimized by a family member (the persecutor) and reaches out to a third family member seeking a rescuer to confide in and/or confront the persecutor. These roles will rotate within the family depending on family emotional health, conflict, drama, and capacity to be aware.

Perfectionist gifted individuals, in my opinion, are susceptible to a pattern of stepping into the rescuer role because they are good problem-solvers and do not want to be perceived as a persecutor or victim. But in triangulation, if we intervene from this point we ultimately disempower the victim even further, thus taking on a persecutor role of sorts.

One way to break this detrimental cycle is to empower the victim to directly address their concerns with the perceived persecutor. You can help them practice what they wish to say. However, if there is a safety issue, you must work to help everyone be safe, so this may not be the best course of action.

Another practical step you can take is to observe how this triangle pattern may be present in other areas of your family, work, and social life, and begin, with this awareness, to step out of the confusion of this dynamic.

Reflection as a Parenting Tool

I have noticed that many of the requirements of parenting, such as safety and guidance, leave parents in a position where they are continually monitoring, questioning, and evaluating various components of their children's life, like academic progress, development, athletic and other competitive pursuits, behaviors, entertainment, electronics use, emotional well-being, and social and friendship matters. These are all important areas but—like teachers who have lost time for creativity in order to prepare students for mandated testing (see chapter 6)—parents, in an effort to keep their children moving forward in our culture, have lost the time, space, and relational ease to just be with their children.

I suggest that you use the tool of reflection to reclaim this time and space for your relationship with your child. As we manage busy lives and households, it is easy to jump right to problem-solving when something is off (or celebration when something is on) for our children and other family members. Reflection gives us another option to weave into the conversation and experience, deepening the connection and relationship in the long run. Reflection is the key to opening wide the doors to communication with your child. It is a bridge you can build now that will be there during the teen and young adult years when children are more independent but still need a reflective checkpoint.

Two Ways to Reflect

My favorite way to teach parents how to reflect is inspired by the work of Bernard and Louise Guerney, who developed Filial Therapy (Guerney 1964), which guides parents to interact with their children in a reflective way that is similar to how child-centered therapists conduct play sessions. Parents learn how to develop the parent and child relationship by learning to follow the child's lead in play that also has structure. Through this simple process, behaviors of concern tend to also shift or fall away as the child is more fully seen and heard (Guerney and Ryan 2013).

When we reflect for children, they can clearly tell we are hearing them and seeing them, in essence, tracking or following their lead. You do not have to be playing with a child to follow their lead and reflect for them; you can do this in ordinary life and within everyday relational exchanges. And, in my experience, the outcomes are consistently magical and illuminating. The hardest part for parents is shifting into this gear and knowing what to say and how to say it. It is particularly difficult for parents who tend to ask their child many questions as their go-to communication route. It may also feel "off" or inauthentic at first to you and maybe even to your child but keep at it and find your own way. You can let your child know you are trying something new if they ask.

There are two ways to reflect that I find are helpful for parents to learn and offer their children: content reflection and feelings reflection.

In content reflection you are tracking what a child is doing or saying and reflecting it back to the child either word for word, or in a summary statement. It is as simple as that.

Here are some word-for-word examples:

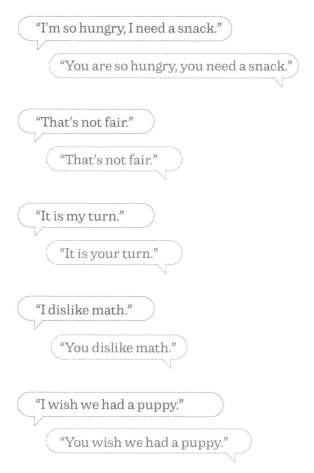

"I'm so hungry, I need a snack."

"You are so hungry, you need a snack."

"That's not fair."

"That's not fair."

"It is my turn."

"It is your turn."

"I dislike math."

"You dislike math."

"I wish we had a puppy."

"You wish we had a puppy."

Can you see how simple this is, yet so challenging to not step right in and talk about how you packed a perfectly good snack, or how you disagree about the fairness of a situation, or talk about why it's not really true about disliking math, or the reasons why your family can't have a puppy?

Here is another example:

"I hate school, we never do anything new."

"You hate school. You never do anything new."

Notice with this example if you had any other responses you wanted to bring forward, like:

"Oh, that's not true."

"You're exaggerating."

"I can talk with your teacher about this tomorrow."

"Tell me about it, that is how I feel about my work most days."

"But you love your teacher."

Here are some other content reflection summary examples:

"Sarah, I noticed you were quiet when you got into the car after school."

"Charlie, it looked like you tried a few different ways to explain that idea to your younger brother."

"Sarah, you seemed to carefully choose the materials you wanted to use on your project."

"Charlie, I noticed you jumped right up and went outside to say hello when you saw our neighbor's dog walk by."

"Sarah, it looked like you and your friend had less to talk about today on the ride home from school."

As parents you are tasked with keeping things running well, and it is natural to move right to questions and solutions. With reflection, you let your child know that you see and hear them. Additionally, you open the door wider for your child to be understood, which will eventually lead to conversation and, hopefully, resolutions.

FEELINGS REFLECTION

The second type of reflection, feelings reflection, is done by taking guesses on how your child might be feeling. I find it is best to guess feelings a child may be experiencing versus telling a child how they are feeling. When we reflect in this way, we are helping the child to clarify their feelings vocabulary and experiences and honoring their inner world. Here are some examples:

"Charlie, I am going to guess you might be feeling sad after having to say goodbye to your grandmother when we headed home."

"Sarah, when you found out you were not invited to her birthday party, I am going to guess you felt sadness, confusion, and maybe even anger."

As is highlighted in these last examples, reflection is sometimes all we can do well when a child is experiencing a tough situation. It lets them know we are trying to understand. Furthermore, it gently demonstrates that we are right there with them versus trying to downplay or distract them from their deep feelings.

It is also okay if your child does not respond to you after you reflect. I find this can take a bit of time at first. The benefit of waiting is that your child begins to clarify how they are feeling and what they are experiencing. Allow them to correct your reflections; know that this will deepen your relationship in the long run, which is especially important groundwork that will be helpful later as they enter their teen years.

This communication tool can feel awkward and feigned at first. It seems obvious to us (but not to children) that we are tracking at this level and it feels clunky to say our observations out loud. I can assure you, once you find your way with this process your child will experience your witnessing of them at an enhanced level. They will be more open to share with you if they know your first response will not be further inquiry, overreaction, a countering opinion, or problem-solving, but will instead be simply validating presence.

Finding Calm

Gifted people tend to live in their thoughts, and a bit in the *ethers*, if they are empathically wired. In my experience, this plus other sensitivities and intensities can actually take them out of their bodies, so to speak, leaving a sense of groundlessness. This unrooted sense can underpin emotional distress, including anxiety. Calming the nervous system through meditation can be helpful, yet you need to be discerning as you introduce this to your child and family. There are many paths and methods to try and for some bright people meditation can feel disorienting, perhaps worsening the distress. There are two authors who have developed this work for children that I recommend: Kathy Hegberg's excellent FocusedKids work, books, and program, and Susan Kaiser Greenland's Inner Kids approach and books. You can find more information on their work in the Resources section.

Parental Self-Care

Parenting a gifted child can be exhausting and so self-care is critical. This can mean different things to different people, but in essence self-care is finding ways to take excellent care of yourself so you can lead a vibrant life on the sunny days and a steady, grounded life on the rainy days.

Of course, nutrition, sleep, exercise, and meaningful social connection is important, but you may find you need more. It will be important to find and nurture your own interests with the same care you nurture your child's interests.

It can also be helpful to commit to practices that you love as well as cultivate relationships with professionals who can help your self-care efforts like body work, counseling, and coaching.

Establishing connection with other parents of gifted children can be helpful to see you are not alone. There are many in-person and online free or low-cost opportunities to connect with other parents.

Parenting high-needs kids can affect any solid parental partnership, but it is possible, with a sense of humor, to create awareness and renewed strength within a partnership as a result of this dynamic.

Deciding who you let into your life is important as well. Empathic gifted people can sometimes find themselves in friendship with people who are draining. If you are in this position, you are at risk for depleting your energy even more.

Have a go-to plan to recharge that honors your introvert or extrovert nature as frequently as you are able.

CHAPTER FOUR

Healthy Habits for Gifted Families

Parents find their way to my counseling office for several primary reasons. One of these is dishar- mony at home within the family and parent-child relationship. In the last chapter we took a look at common gifted family dynamics and ways to support yourself and your child in these instances.

In this chapter, we will explore more deeply how to form a foundation as a gifted family to prevent or weather most storms. In particular, we will look at healthy communication techniques and practices.

Asking for What You Need

Mentioned briefly in the last chapter, this method of encouraging children to ask directly for what they need is fairly easy to implement and provides a great foundation for gifted children to experience themselves as effective self-advocates. Parents, especially perfectionistic first-time parents, often have a harder time stepping aside to let their children ask directly for what they need as they become capable of doing so. A pattern develops where children come to depend entirely on their parents to get their needs met, short-circuiting their ability to answer for themselves or ask for what they need directly. Children will then begin to seek out what they need through indirect ways, which can translate to behavior concerns like sneakiness, fibbing, or passive personality development. With this pattern, later challenges around school advocacy and even personal safety in the teen years can emerge.

Here is how you can start this practice: Whenever your child asks for what they need or desire, no matter how small the request, no matter your answer, say first:

Thank you for asking for what you need.

This response lets children know you are listening and appreciate their agency or natural bent toward being independent. Taking these steps and hearing this feedback is important to their development.

If your child is unable to ask for what they need directly, help them along at first. Watch your child's cues that indicate they want something, which you ordinarily respond to by meeting their need. In this moment, instead say:

Charlie, it looks like you are wishing for me to help you find your house key. I am happy to help you, just ask. Say, "Mom, can you help me find my house key?"

Healthy Parent Communication Basics: What Not to Say, and How Not to Say It

After over 20 years of counseling families through some challenging matters, I have seen what tends to work and what doesn't. Here are a few guidelines that can steer you toward meaningful exchanges and away from unproductive or detrimental conversations with your children.

▶ Transpose all sarcasm into kind humor; jokes should not be mean-spirited or at the child's expense. If you are not able to do this, drop the sarcasm altogether.

▶ Do not talk negatively about your child, your partner, or any other family members in front of your child, or within earshot of your child. This is critically important if parents are separated or divorced.

▶ Do not lie to your children. If for some good reasons you cannot discuss the specifics of something with them, tell them this in a general way: *Charlie, I would like to answer your question, but I can't right now; it is complicated (or you are not old enough, or it is an adult concern, etc.). If/when I am able to share more with you, I will.*

▶ Turn off your phone or do not look at or answer your phone/text/email when you are in a conversation with your child.

▶ If you are angry, name your emotion and advise your child you need a moment to regroup. Return to the conversation as soon as you are able.

▶ Do not put off or avoid having a conversation unnecessarily. If you have indicated it is not a good time to talk, make sure you come back to have the conversation as soon as you can.

- If your child has asked for your confidence, and you cannot honor this, do not promise to do so. Instead, say, *Sarah, I cannot promise this. I may need to share what you share with me with your dad.*
- If you need to apologize, apologize. Do not rationalize your actions. Do not give excuses.
- When your child is struggling with something, it is unhelpful to talk about your own struggles in a comparative way. For example: *You think you have it bad, listen to what happened to me. You think you are disappointed in your grades, imagine how I feel?*
- When you offer a reflection to your child, it is okay for them to not respond right away or at all.
- Do not drink or use any other impairing substances when in difficult or important conversations with your child. Request that you speak the next day, when you have a clear mind.
- No blaming: *If you hadn't taken so long to get in the car, this would not have happened to us.*
- No shaming: *You are old enough to know better.*
- Do not admonish your child in front of friends, siblings, extended family, neighbors, teachers, coaches, or other parents, or in public. If it is a safety concern, like they ran across a busy street, and you react publicly out of concern, once home and calm debrief this with your child, explaining your fear and concern.
- Accept and reflect all of your child's feelings. Do not demand they snap out of anger, frustration, stubbornness, and the like.
- If your marriage or partnership is struggling, do not substitute your child for emotional support or other needs.
- If your child's ideas or interests are different from yours, do not dismiss them.
- Do not speak for your child.

- Do not assume silence means no response. Ask your child if they need more time to collect their thoughts.
- Do not demand your child look you in the eye during conversations to demonstrate respect or prove they are listening, particularly boys. They are listening (Pollack 1999).
- Do not triangulate in other people during a challenging matter with your child or partner. Speak directly with the person you are in conflict with (see Triangulation on page 69).
- Watch how your birth order shows up in challenging circumstances and conversations. For example, if you were the youngest child in your family, you may be activated when your oldest child excludes your youngest child. Own and sort out this projection.
- As discussed earlier, get in touch with what feelings live underneath your anger, so you can communicate a more accurate assessment of your emotions, and open up more meaningful dialogue. Over time, this will help your child be better able to articulate what they are feeling, too.

Supporting Your Child: Encouragement Versus Praise

When parents encourage a child, they send a message that they see their child's specific efforts and progress and are rooting for them, no matter what—win, lose, or otherwise. With encouragement, we are offering support to children that fortifies their development of intrinsic motivation (see Two Types of Motivation on page 94) and self-esteem and fosters healthy risk-taking. Encouragement can also insulate a child from developing a (high) need for approval.

When parents praise a child, they send a message of external approval or judgment that has to do with behaviors and outcomes the parents see as desirable. Since it can initially feel good to receive praise, children may become focused on gaining their parents' approval in this way. When this happens, the child's ability to develop intrinsic motivation is diminished and their need for approval can become fortified. This is an especially difficult position for a perfectionistic gifted child.

Once you learn and practice the difference, you will begin to notice how pervasive praise is in our culture and education system. It is such an important facet to understand as a parent, but it can be confusing. Why wouldn't we want to praise children? Well, when we do, we can set a child up to seek approval outside of themselves and this can undercut their development. This is especially true for perfectionistic children. Praise phrases like "good job" also do not offer room to acknowledge how much effort a child undertook or progress a child has made. When we encourage instead, we can become specific about what we notice and this will both hold more meaning for the child and take our external approval out of the equation. For example, for a child who is learning to swim you might name how you see them trying to figure out each of the different stroke and kick patterns. Or, you see how much preparation and courage it might have taken to jump into the deep end of the pool for the first time. When we praise, we shortcut the relational and supportive benefits of encouragement while creating a dependence on us for approval that will be difficult to untangle later.

Statements like these might fall under encouragement:

▶ I noticed you worked for a long time trying to figure that out.
▶ I watched as it seemed you made a thoughtful choice.

- I saw how you figured out a way to talk about that difficult incident and apologize.
- You could have just given up, but you stayed with it and kept trying.

Statements like this fall under praise:

- Good job.
- Nice work.
- You rocked it.
- I like the way you did your homework.
- You did what I asked, like a good boy.

Can you see and feel the difference? When we support a gifted child's internal efforts through encouragement we free them up to learn and interact well with the world with less fear of failure. This will strengthen their sense of self and their natural drive toward making their way well in this world under their own terms and power.

When we praise instead of encourage gifted children, we place them at risk, because we are undercutting the development of their ability to motivate themselves and putting them at the mercy of external approval. Potentially, these children can suffer greatly in their teen years and young adulthood because they have not lived for themselves yet, and will continue to seek external validation.

It is certainly all right to offer praise in moments of celebration and haste, but you need to circle back to reflecting your child's efforts. For example, if your child wins the spelling bee or a snowboard half-pipe event or rides their bike for the first time without training wheels, you most likely will only have time in that excited moment to say something like a praise statement—that is okay. Just ground this excitement later with your child by reflecting and highlighting what you noticed about their focus, their motivation, their practice, their perseverance, and maybe even the courage it took to try.

Parents Are in Charge

Sometimes gifted children wish to be in charge of family operations, including discipline of younger siblings. This can emerge naturally and also from parents asking older children to step in to supervise younger children, especially if parents are feeling stressed out and count on a mature older sibling to give them a break.

If this is happening in your home, I suggest you work to correct this as soon as you can. Find parenting or counseling support for yourself and communicate to your child that as the parent it is your responsibility, not theirs, to provide the supervision and guidance of other children in your family. Be available to them as they discuss their frustration with siblings. You may learn of circumstances that need your attention and need to be addressed.

How long this dynamic has been present will determine how difficult it will be to shift. In my experience, if this goes unaddressed and continues, it is the family version of when gifted advanced learners are asked by their classroom teacher to put their own learning aside to help other classmates, who end up resenting them anyway. Childhood is short, but the impact is life-long; we do not want gifted children to miss the window of being children, nor do we want this dynamic to potentially damage sibling relationships.

I am not suggesting that children do not have a voice or responsibilities at home. As part of their family membership, it is important that gifted children's experiences and ideas are honored. Nor am I advising that parents need to rule their home in an authoritarian (Baumrind 1967) or punitive manner. It is important, however, that gifted children feel they live in a safely predictable family structure that they can count on as they develop and grow.

Family Rules and Consequences

Once you and your partner are committed to align your parenting (see Get on the Same Parenting Page on page 53) it is helpful to put a few rules in place. It is best to construct rules and consequences together with your children, so everyone has a chance to reflect and discuss.

It is important to keep this process simple. Setting a hundred rules will overwhelm everyone and undermine the intention. It will also lead to potential rule loopholes, creating more work for you as a parent in the end.

If you are a family across two homes, your child will benefit if the same rules, even if they differ a bit, are largely in place in both homes. In my training and experience I have learned you only need two or three rules (Hegberg, 2002):

① In this home, parents are in charge.

> Talk about this together from a health and safety perspective. For example, parents set the safety parameters and will continue to do so throughout a child's growing-up years. Also, discuss how this does not mean parents are autocrats; children will have an important voice. But at the end of the day, parents are in charge to help everyone stay safe.

② In this home, we treat one another with respect and kindness.

> Talk about what respect and kindness mean to each family member and what everyone needs to feel they are being treated with respect and kindness and commit to supporting everyone in this way. For example, if your eight-year-old needs your four-year-old to stay out of their room unsupervised, make this clear to the younger child and back your eight-year-old up.

③ In this home, we each have responsibilities.

> This rule is optional but can cover whatever needs to be accomplished individually for the greater good of the family. Responsibilities like work, homework, chores, and pet care fall under this rule. If your children have chores, I recommend this be outlined on a separate, posted, chore list.

How to Make Rules and Consequences Work

To begin this process, set up a family meeting (more on this in the next section).

Bring art supplies and ask the children to draw up a simple rules chart based on the three previous rules. At my office we keep it simple with a sheet of standard printer paper, usually placing a *rules* column on the left and a *consequences* column on the right. Don't worry about spelling errors and messiness in the crafting of the chart; let your child take the lead in this part, if they wish. Make it clear that these rules apply to each and every family member, including parents. If you need help remembering what everyone needs to feel respected or how they define kindness, create side lists for every family member to post next to the rules, including reminders like "No Name Calling." Let children help decide a private place where the chart should hang in your home. It's important to make your gifted child a co-author in this process.

Next, you must decide on two sets of consequences for breaking the rules: one for children, and one for parents. In my experience, the consequences children wish most for their parents is a meaningful apology plus more dedicated time together—like one extra hour of reading together, each evening, for one week. Also, children generally have a sense of an appropriate consequence for themselves, usually something like less screen time. If you or your child are finding it difficult to come up with consequences together, you can certainly take the lead and create the consequences. However, they will most likely not be heeded nor adopted by your child.

One way to foster your child's participation is to give them plenty of time to think this consequence part through. Maybe the first meeting simply establishes what the first two rules look like, and what respect and kindness look like for each family member. Then set a second meeting date a week or so later to discuss consequences. This may take time. Creating family rules is not a quick-fix strategy, but it will become part of your family culture so take all the time you need to launch this process well.

One last word of advice: Do not threaten a consequence unnecessarily to enforce or shepherd an outcome you desire. For example, if your family has been invited to a wedding, and your child does not feel comfortable wearing a necktie or scratchy (to them) dress, pause. Instead of threatening the consequence they contributed to the family rules, talk this situation through with them. In this case, the feedback you get will most likely guide you later to plan ahead for your child to feel comfortable in similar circumstances. For example, the discomfort in scratchy clothes can be an indicator a pediatric occupational therapy evaluation might be helpful.

Family Meetings

I recommend organizing a standing family meeting and creating a format that is lovely, fun, and follows a predictable agenda. I think a weekly meeting is best. It can work to have a check-in where every family member has a turn to share what's working for them within the family and what's not working for them within the family, and brainstorm ways to work together to overcome challenges.

Mix in a good snack and use the time together to build a wonderful family tradition, like

- ▶ Reciting a favorite poem.
- ▶ A one-song dance party to your family's favorite song.
- ▶ Highlighting a different throwback family photo each week.
- ▶ Coordinating an appreciation circle where everyone says something they appreciate about everyone else.
- ▶ Taking turns offering acknowledgments for family members who have contributed to one another's or the family's well-being.
- ▶ Offering acknowledgment of a family member's progress or efforts toward accomplishing a goal they have set for themself.

You can spend a few moments talking about special plans like ideas for a family game night menu, or summer travel, or preparing for an upcoming family birthday. You can also discuss other matters that have come up during the week that need to be discussed more fully.

I strongly caution against turning this family connection into a time that will be experienced by the children as punishment, admonishment, or complaints about their behaviors. This is about communication, becoming more attuned to one another, supporting one another, and being together. If you want to use family meeting time to craft family rules, I advise you wait until you have had a number of wonderful meeting experiences before you take this step.

Just like a work meeting, you can create a simple agenda that becomes a family tradition.

See the example below.

Our Family Meeting Schedule

TONIGHT'S SNACK MENU: APPLES AND GLUTEN-FREE CHOCOLATE CHIP COOKIES

First order of business	▶ Sharing and talking about tonight's Throwback Family Photo
What is working well in our household right now?	Each member can add to this part of the meeting, things like: ▶ Having backpacks packed the night before school. ▶ Adding new veggie lasagna recipe to the family meal rotation. ▶ Everyone washing their hands before dinner. ▶ Working together on an anniversary surprise for grandparents.
What's not working well in our household right now? Brainstorm possible solutions	▶ Consistently feeding the new puppy on time. (Let's set reminders on our phones.) ▶ Everyone needing computer access at the same time. (Create school night schedule.)
Other business	▶ Baking cupcakes for new neighbors. ▶ Planning family visit to art museum. ▶ Close with appreciation circle.

CHAPTER FIVE

Motivation and Conflict Resolution

Two of the common challenges parents of gifted children face are addressing motivational concerns and emotional, high-intensity outbursts. While this chapter offers some insights and strategies for resolving these issues, if you're still struggling, I strongly encourage you to revisit chapter 3 (on page 51) as it delves into some core issues that may be manifesting themselves through the behaviors discussed in this chapter.

Supporting the development of your gifted child's healthy motivation will pay off. In their youth, your child will be happier and better able to focus on interests they find fulfilling. As they grow up, they will have better self-understanding and be prepared to succeed in more self-directed learning and work environments.

Motivation Basics

From my experience, I see much confusion for parents surrounding their child's motivation. Parents wish for their gifted children to be successful in life, but intuitively they can also feel the toll of perfectionism and the taxing effects of high achievement on their children. Further compounding this tension is when children are underachieving, appear to have lost motivation, or are perceived by educators as working below their potential.

Whether gifted or not, there are two main ways humans are motivated: intrinsically and extrinsically. Knowing how your child is currently motivated is crucial for aiding their development.

Two Types of Motivation

Intrinsic motivation is motivation that comes from within us and moves us toward the life we wish to create, the experiences we wish to have, the learning we wish to explore, and accomplishments we are interested in pursuing.

Extrinsic motivation involves being motivated by something outside of the self. For children, these external motivators are typically rewards and punishments tied to behavior and performance. Alfie Kohn outlined the detrimental impact of rewards and punishments in school to motivation—and in parenting, as it undercuts the child's self-esteem and development as well as the parent-child relationship (Kohn 1993, 2005).

Intrinsically motivated individuals may work toward goals that lead to external recognition, but the recognition itself does not generally drive their internal motivation. Instead, what moves them forward might be learning something new or mastering a skill. In my experience, when gifted children feel accepted for who they are and what is important to them—and have the freedom to falter in the service of their pursuits without judgment or criticism—it is easier for them to work from a place of intrinsic motivation.

Extrinsically motivated individuals may also have to reckon with a high need to achieve, or a fear of failure. Some gifted people experience a need to achieve that is so strong, it can preclude taking any healthy risks and, paradoxically, leads to underachievement.

When gifted youth become oriented around external motivators like grades and rankings, once through their education they may be at risk of crash-and-burn experiences when required to be more independent in their workplaces and at other adult pursuits.

Culturally we prize awards, recognition, good grades, and promotions, but if a person is primarily motivated by what is outside of themselves, there is always risk. Like much of what we have discussed in this book, there is a paradox here. On the surface, it looks like high achievement can lead a gifted child or teen to some wonderful places—awards, top grades, recognition. This is true, but below the surface the reality is that being externally motivated with a high need to achieve or a fear of failure can be costly to self-esteem, development, and adult functioning.

Why the Sudden Lack of Motivation?

Gifted children don't usually start out having a lack of motivation with learning, especially as they start school. So parents feel understandably baffled and concerned when a gifted child suddenly switches course. In my experience, the reasons gifted children and adolescents can lose steam or, worse, give up altogether, are varied. Here are the most common reasons I see for a lack of motivation:

- Undiagnosed, and thus unaddressed, twice- or multi-exceptionality

- Acute perfectionism leading to underachievement
- Meaningless, uninteresting, irrelevant, or redundant school content
- Teaching practices or classroom culture a mismatch for the child
- Competition in the classroom or school culture
- School, classroom, or family uses a behavioral or *rewards-and-punishments* approach
- Intolerable social environment at school
- Self-esteem concerns born of critical or high-achieving parents
- Parental addiction, personality disorder, mood disorder, escalated anger, or a history of abuse (physical, emotional, or sexual) or neglect, or other considerable stress in the home environment
- Unaddressed depression or anxiety
- A preference for failing on their own terms
- Anger with the educational and/or family system
- Parental focus on grades versus meaningful learning
- Success may lead to more pressure
- Feeling unseen or unheard
- Ideas or interests are not taken seriously, nor woven into education
- Sees adult life, or life generally, as existentially futile
- Trying to fit in better with peers
- Study skills undeveloped from earlier years, when they were unneeded
- Unspoken family pressure to not outshine parents

I encourage you to review this list and see how many of these may fit what you see in your child. Diagnosing the issue is only part of the solution, of course. We cover some proactive parenting strategies in the next section that can help. Troubles with the school environment and curriculum should also be addressed with your child's educator. For more on how to work with teachers and school staff, see chapter 7 (page 127).

Preventing Motivation Concerns and Rekindling Motivation

There are a few key steps you can take to prevent a decline in your child's motivation. And, fortunately, it is also possible to help guide your gifted child to reestablish healthy motivation. In my experience, preventing motivation issues is far easier than trying to reset motivation later in a child or teen's life.

If you want your child to be more motivated because you want them to achieve rather than fail, I can't help you. What I can offer is a path moving away from the pitfalls of high achievement and fear of failure, and toward more meaningful exchanges with your child, a deepened parent and child relationship, authentic learning, and a healthy shift allowing breathing room for your child's intrinsic motivation to take root and develop.

As is often my guidance, it can be helpful to first self-reflect. As a start, think through how you feel about these ideas:

① Determine your motivation and achievement stances. If you or your child's other parent have a high need to achieve and a high fear of failure, and are driven by motivators outside of yourself, you will need to begin to support your own growth in this area before you can truly assist your child.

② In the service of your child's happiness, can you tolerate an alternate route that may not look *perfect* in the mainstream view?

Here are practical ideas and strategies to move the motivation needle:

Practicing Encouragement and Reflection, Not Rewards and Punishments

As we discussed earlier, it's vital to become practiced at giving encouragement rather than praise (see page 83) and learn to be reflective in parenting your children (see page 71) to promote their development and deepen your parent-child relationship. These practices will assist your child in cultivating a more effortless, natural initiative and motivation. It is also critical to move away from rewards (bribes, incentives, etc.) and punishment (including punitive actions that take away a child's sense of safety) to control behaviors and outcomes. Punishments and rewards are part of a "doing-to versus working-with" parenting orientation; they do not work and will only worsen outcomes and your relationship (Kohn 1993, 2005).

This approach does not mean that you disregard concerns that need to be addressed, but rather that you learn how to approach these dilemmas in a non-punitive way that will truly support your child and your relationship. If you need more guidance on making this shift, I recommend reading Alfie Kohn's book *Unconditional Parenting* (2005).

In leaving bribes and rewards behind, you can still surprise or treat your child, but do not tie these generous gestures to performance, achievement, or good behavior. Marking an important event like a completion of a big project or high school graduation can of course be celebrated, but do not bribe or incentivize your child to complete these milestones. You can still recognize accomplishment but use reflection to describe to your child what you saw in their process, which encourages them. For example: *I saw how frustrating the group work was at points of this project, and I watched as you tried to communicate your concerns, even though your project team wasn't open to the feedback.*

Another way you can turn this ship around is engaging your child. When your gifted child asks you if you like their work, instead of offering your opinion ask how *they* feel about their work. Here are some reflective starting points:

▶ Ask them to tell you about what they have created.
▶ Ask them to tell you what part of the work was most important or meaningful to them and why.
▶ Ask how they decided to approach the assignments.
▶ Ask them to reflect on what they might have done differently in the process.

When you want to offer your thoughts on their work or constructive feedback that may be experienced by your child as criticism, preface your comments by letting them know there is something you noticed that you want to share but it may be hard for them to hear. Let your child know it is not your intention to hurt their feelings, but instead to help. Be specific, sensitive, and kindhearted in your remarks.

If you or others in your family tree have a highly critical nature, actively try to shift this. Criticism will not work, and it will undermine your parent-child relationship. The same is true of being highly-demanding. Demands also do not work, and they will also undermine your parent-child relationship. Reflect on your own relationship to authority and how it impacts how you feel about yourself, your gifted child, their accomplishments, and their reflection on you and your accomplishments.

Acknowledge Interests, Fortify Character

Know your child's major interests, as well as what changes day-to-day, and support these at home. Work to weave their interests into their educational landscape as well. If your gifted child is uninterested in developing skills or focusing on one content area, find a way to develop this area using something that is interesting to them.

- Find ways to share interests with your gifted child. If the interest is something you are already skilled in, talk about this with your child before you begin the endeavor. Remind them that you were in the same beginning place when you started, and you understand if they feel like it is challenging. Discuss in advance, or in the moment, what they need to feel comfortable. Let your child tell you; don't jump in right away. Remember, you are there to help and support them, not tell them exactly what to do.

- Find things both of you can struggle to learn together. Understand mistakes are part of learning anything and allow this to be a primary message for yourself and your home. When something goes wrong, or you make a mistake, show your child how kindheartedly you can live and learn with it.

- When playing board and other games with very young children, we might, as they are learning, try to encourage them by letting them win. Young gifted children understand at some point when this is happening and it may undercut their inner drive to learn. It also sets the stage for a childhood of bending rules. Although letting children win games they enjoy or are just learning is well-intended, it is best, in my experience, to try to play card and board games by the rules, fair and square, with gifted children. This gives children practice with perseverance, especially when playing a game with an element of chance. Let young children know they will become more skillful as they become older; this is part of growing up. Acknowledge and reflect when your child has persevered through a game setback to catch up or get ahead. Acknowledge their sportsmanship as well, when it is present during the intensity of the setback.

Evaluate the Learning Environment

When gifted children are in the wrong learning environment, this needs to be addressed. We will discuss this further in chapter 7.

► Gut-check the school choice you have made and if it feels off, work to establish what is not working and what your child needs.

► If this is not possible, make adjustments, even if it means moving out of your neighborhood school (see chapter 7).

► If you hire a tutor to support your child in an under-motivated area, I advise you to find someone who uses a different learning approach than the classroom teacher. Otherwise, you may be doubling down on the possible unmotivating factor.

► Find mentors for your gifted child to work with, particularly in their interest areas. Sometimes these individuals can help young people see and develop their capacities in different ways while sharing knowledge about your child's interest areas.

► As we discussed in chapter 1, if a child is struggling and uninterested in certain school subjects or content areas, research possible twice-exceptionality and consider having your child evaluated for intervention.

Listen to What Your Child Is Telling You

Help your gifted child feel empowered by taking them seriously when they discuss their frustrations, needs, and ideas. Here are some examples of ways you can support your child this way.

- When gifted children tell us they want to do something themselves, they do. Allow this to happen. There may be times when, for safety reasons, you will need to help them until they are old enough to do something by themselves.
- Give your gifted child space and freedom to express frustrations by listening to and reflecting on what they are telling you.
- If there is someone who your child says they enjoy learning and working with at school, ask if there are interests they may enjoy working on together outside of school and then make arrangements for this to happen.
- Ask your child to identify and help create a workspace that meets their needs, taking into account noise, lighting, furniture, and community.
- If you offer to help your gifted child with their work, or if they ask you to help them with their work, first ask your child what is actually helpful and then discuss how your child wants you to intervene, or not. Listen carefully to what your child is telling you and don't take it personally; see it instead as self-advocacy on the child's part and respond kindheartedly. Have a communication plan, so during your work together your child has a way to communicate if something is not working.

Procrastination

Many gifted people, of all ages, have a tendency to procrastinate. If this is true for you, you may find your child's procrastination especially painful to witness, and I have two recommendations for you.

First, consider your relationship to electronic school-based homework and grade tracking systems to monitor your child's progress. If you have a procrastinating child, daily use of these systems will find you in conflict and power struggles that are unnecessary. Instead, limit your use of these systems to once per week—a day of the week of your child's choosing—and set up a regular way to meet with your child to discuss their school workload with them directly. Let them know you trust them to discuss this honestly with you, and they can count on you not to overreact.

Secondly, because many gifted children actually wait until right before a deadline or the very end of the term to complete and hand in their work, your time can be better spent helping them become aware of what they need to support themselves in their procrastination rather than trying to change their natures.

In my practice, I call the culmination of this advice and process *homework amnesty*. A homework amnesty process requires a gifted student to come clean about falling way behind and select a day to catch up, along with selecting all of the other supports they will need. Things I ask gifted young people to consider and plan out with their parents in advance of the *homework amnesty* day include:

- What time do they want to wake up?
- How do they want to wake up?
- What is for breakfast?
- What time does work start?
- Where in the house do they want to work?

- What time are their breaks, including lunch?
- What is for lunch?
- How long is lunch, and other breaks?
- What snacks need to be available, and when?
- What materials and supplies do they need?
- Do they want family members to visit or check in on them? If so, how?
- What time will they finish?
- How will they celebrate, with their family, the work they have completed?

As we discussed with rules and consequences in the previous chapter, allowing children to have a role in this structure makes it exponentially easier to gain their genuine commitment to the plan. Your job is to help provide what was requested and trust your child will follow through.

Supporting Gifted Children Through Outbursts

As we have reviewed so far, gifted children, like gifted adults, are intense, sensitive, and perfectionistic, and have a strong sense of justice. This mixture of characteristics often creates the perfect conditions for you and your child both to have a low threshold for circumstances leading to escalated arguments, outbursts, spinouts, conflict, meltdowns, or whatever your family calls it.

When it is you who is outbursting, it is your job to get to the bottom of your distress, find a way into balance, and co-regulate with your family members. Otherwise, your outbursts will undercut your child's capacity to develop and thrive.

Most gifted people benefit from working with a counselor to sort out their intensity and other related matters at some point. However, many gifted adults have struggled to find a clinician who is gifted and understands giftedness, in order to truly be able to help. Stigma and gifted perfectionism also keep many gifted adults away from this kind of support for themselves and their children. Reflect honestly on whether you struggle with intensity and, if so, seek proper support.

When your child is outbursting, they are letting you know something is off. Your job as a parent is to help your child get to the bottom of their distress and find their way back into balance with themselves and co-regulation with you and family members.

A Simple Process to Support

I hope the following strategy offers a starting point to help you and your child kindly get to the heart of what is underneath outbursts, as well as lessen their frequency and soften their intensity over time. Depending on the age of your child, it may be difficult for you to see the progress right away, because a family pattern of behavior has developed over the years, and it will take time to unwind this patterning. Part of this patterning will most likely include your own intensity, sensitivity, perfectionism, and experiences as a child, and these will need to be untangled by you in order for this process to work.

This process, if consistently offered by a parent from a place of sincerely wishing to help, often works:

① When your child goes into distress, do what you can to not go into distress yourself. Stay grounded and non-defensive—and remember that your child feels safe enough to lose it with you, which is the highest compliment they can pay you (Hegberg 2002). It is your responsibility to help your child figure this out.

② Do not ignore your child (Kohn 2005).

③ Let them know you can see they have something important they are trying to tell you and that you want to hear all about it when they are calmer and ready to tell you.

④ Let them know you are there, but until things are a bit calmer it isn't possible to understand, listen, and figure things out together.

⑤ Do not send your child away. If they wish to go to another room of your home, that is okay.

⑥ Let them know you will keep checking in with them to see when they are ready to connect and discuss. Let them know they can take all the time they need; you will be right there or nearby.

⑦ Stay nearby and keep checking in with your child as they continue to settle and calm.

⑧ When you check in, you can say: *Are you ready yet? No, not ready. That's okay, I'll keep checking.* Or, *Are you ready? Great, let's sit down and talk. Where shall we meet? Do you need anything?* Offer suggestions: tissues, a few minutes of no talking together, a drink of water, a hug, etc.

⑨ Once you have gotten to this point, hear your child out and reflect back what they are upset about. I recommend you do not become defensive. Just listen sincerely.

I advise you to also let your child know how much you appreciate being able to discuss these matters together. Remind them that being intense and figuring out conflicts is part of being human, part of growing up, and part of being gifted. You will get through this together. This will greatly help a perfectionistic gifted child, especially one who is embarrassed about the incident.

If your child has brought up something sincere in this conversation that needs to be addressed, do so the next day. Circle back during a private and calm time: *I was thinking about our talk yesterday when you told me it feels unfair... I am going to watch this more. I appreciate you telling me. Can you let me know next time, if I don't notice it?*

During this debrief time, you can also reflect back to your child any strides they/you are making in this area: *Sarah, it seems it is getting easier for us both to find more calm, figure things out together, and have these conversations.*

THERE ARE NO "BAD" FEELINGS

When gifted children show us their intensity in the form of anger, sadness, or anxiety, it can be challenging to hold steady as a parent. Your own intense experiences of concern, fear, or frustration can be activated, and you may feel stuck, unequipped, or out of control.

In my experience, what is most helpful to know in these moments is that although your child's expressions of their feelings may be intense, there is something important your child is trying to tell you. This one awareness, like a quick sip of cool water on the hottest summer day, can engage your ability to respond lovingly, safely, and effectively if you let it.

You will need to wait until your child has settled down before you can debrief with them to get to the heart of the matter. While you are waiting for the calm, it is best not to send your child away as this may feel like love withdrawal (Kohn 2005), but instead let your child know you see they are trying to tell you something important, you are in it with them, and you will be there for them no matter what.

The complexity of the intensity may be difficult to untangle with your child. Some matters will unfold, and it will be possible to discuss and support your child. However, there are things you must pay attention to as they may require you to seek professional counseling:

- ▸ Inconsolable tearfulness
- ▸ Frequent withdrawal from family, school, activities, and friends
- ▸ Escalating anger
- ▸ Physical lashing out and/or self-harming actions or threats
- ▸ Suicide concerns
- ▸ Statements like: I hate myself, I wish I had never been born, I wish I were dead
- ▸ Changes in sleep, appetite, activity
- ▸ Intense anxiety and worry
- ▸ Out-of-control perfectionism
- ▸ Drug or alcohol consumption
- ▸ Disordered eating
- ▸ A sense of hopelessness
- ▸ Anything else that seems off to you—trust your gut here

Although these circumstances are hard to talk about, they must be acknowledged. Again, your child is trying to tell you something and they need your assistance. Don't sweep these types of concerns under the rug or chalk them up to immaturity or adolescence. Get to the bottom of what your child needs.

CHAPTER SIX

Gifted Friendships and Social Dynamics

Gifted children, adolescents, and teens want meaningful friendships, but it can be challenging to find, establish, and maintain these connections. Research shows gifted children move along a developmental hierarchy of age-related stages, from a simple to more mature expectation and understanding of friendship, ultimately seeking deep, safe connection (Gross, 2001). We also understand that gifted children will be drawn to befriend other gifted children (Hollingworth 1926, Mann 1957, O'Shea 1960, Gross 1993, 2001).

As a parent, watching your child struggle to find true friendship can be stressful. In this chapter, I will give you guidance on how to support your gifted child in this process.

A Good Friend Can
Be Hard to Find

This is especially true for gifted children. With all of the asynchronies, complexities, and specific and special interests to factor in, it may take some time for your child to find a friend, where both children feel the fit. Your child may meet and know children at school or in your neighborhood who they play with but finding true friendship may take time.

In my experience, it is wise to be encouraging but not to build false hope for your children during the wait. For example, if a child is starting a new school year, even in a new gifted program, this does not necessarily mean they will find meaningful friendship. One of the best things you can do if your child hasn't found a true friend yet is to use this wait time to talk about fate and friendship, and how sometimes this can happen in unlikely ways. Here are some useful conversation starters:

- ▸ Discuss qualities of authentic engagement—how it feels to be with someone who understands. Think about your own close childhood friends and how you found each other.
- ▸ Talk about the general characteristics of a good friend—concepts like respect, kindness, trust, and reciprocity. Ask your child to articulate what qualities they think a good friend might have. Discuss what you enjoy about your adult friends and what makes them good friends.
- ▸ Talk about gifted nature—including intensity, perfectionism, and sensitivity—and how these qualities may impact gifted friendship. For example, ask your child: *What if you find a friend who has the same amount or more sensitivity than we do as a family? What if they*

come over to play and need some quiet play, but you are feeling like doing something more active, like building a fort?

▸ Discuss introversion and extroversion, and the related needs that could emerge within friendships. For example, with a social but introverted gifted child who needs downtime to recharge after a school week, you could discuss how to set kind boundaries and plan future play with an extroverted neighborhood friend who likes to stop by a few times every Saturday morning to say hello and hang out.

How to Help Your Gifted Child Find Friends

While it is certainly helpful to engage in thoughtful discussion with your child about friendship and values, it's still challenging to wait for the joy that can come when you have found a true friend. If your child is struggling, this section offers you ideas to consider to help them find children they can connect with, as well as tips on what you can do to help them maintain those vital connections when they've found a potential friend.

Broaden Their Horizons

Track down local and regional programs, activities, and summer camps that match with your child's interests. If you live in an area with gifted programing, find out what is available. There are a number of national gifted summer programs as well as interesting online options. Talk with your child about trying new activities. Stay open to what they wish to pursue; sometimes gifted children are reluctant to tell parents about interests because they diverge from family or parental interests.

Ask your child big open-ended questions to develop these ideas.

- For example, ask: *If you could learn about anything this summer, or experience anything this summer, without any concern about what something costs or where it is located, what would you pick? Where would you go? What would you like to do?*
- Your gifted child may inform you they are interested in something fantastical, but within that vision you can usually find something grounded that can be explored. For example, a child who wishes to go out on tour with a beloved singer-songwriter could enjoy access to a rental keyboard or guitar, perhaps leading to a music lesson or a composition, poetry writing, or song writing workshop.

Help Them Make the Initial Connection

Gifted people of all ages, including children, tend to dislike engaging in small talk or many icebreaker activities. Instead, they want to dive directly into deeper conversation. This can create an extra challenge in taking the first steps of meeting someone new.

It is helpful to teach your child how to simply introduce themselves: *I'm Charlie. What is your name?* Let them know it may be up to them to make the first introduction, and that other kids may not know how to introduce themselves, or even respond, and that this can be part of life and is not necessarily a reflection of them. Help them see it may take time, and a number of attempts, before they get a response or find someone they connect well with.

In my practice, taking a cue from etiquette teachers, I help gifted young people understand that people in general, even introverts, enjoy talking about themselves. They usually just need a good question or two to get the conversation going. I help children craft a couple of go-to questions that they can memorize and have at the ready when they meet someone new who is a potential friend. Brainstorm a few questions with your child and, if it seems helpful, let them practice with you to see how it feels. Try to craft open-ended questions that require more than a yes or no response, and questions that ask about things that are important for your child.

For example:

▶ What got you interested in this camp/activity/class/game/place?
▶ How did you learn so much about activity/class/game/place?
▶ Where do you get your ideas for the stories you write, things that you build, inventions you design?
▶ What are your favorite books, movies, games?

Host a Get-Together

Gifted children, like all children, need your support as they begin to socialize with friends. I have found it is helpful to include gifted children in planning a get-together at your home. I suggest you sit and plan together with your child well in advance of the playdate. Including them in the process at this level will minimize the impact of mishaps and help your child build self-esteem and skills in being a good host. Here are some items you may wish to include in your planning:

▶ Set day, date, and time.
▶ Talk about siblings. How will you as a parent keep them from interfering with the playdate?

- Create a snack menu together and if your child enjoys cooking, choose snacks they can help prepare in advance.
- Set or review simple house boundaries, rules, and agreements, including approved play areas and activities.
- Discuss what it means to host, and what kinds of play options the guest may be interested in.
- Talk about conflict resolution during the playdate (with the friend and siblings).
- Talk about transition timing. What kind of time warning will you give so children can transition well and happily to saying goodbye?
- Plan for a rainy or snowy day, or for a postponement.
- Help your child keep track of their friend's play and other preferences for future get-togethers, in order to help them sample the joy of being a great host.
- Create a way for your child to let you know if something is not working and they need your help.
- Debrief quickly and lovingly after the event to discuss what worked, what didn't work, and what you would do differently in the future. Use this time to reflect for your child what you witnessed that was lovely.
- Follow up together on any loose ends: thank you notes, lost or borrowed items returned, etc.

I suggest you use this same process to discuss your child accepting an invite to play at a friend's home. Try to foresee what could be helpful for your child to feel comfortable, and to be a good guest. Again, have a way for your child to communicate with you if it is not working out and they need your assistance to leave early. This is also an important process to have in place for older, gifted teen children who may find themselves in an uncomfortable social situation.

Keep in Touch

If your child makes a true connection with another child in an activity or program, do what you can to see if the other family is interested in having the children stay connected, even if you live in different places.

- Help your child stay connected through phone calls and letter writing, or vet a safe way to connect the children online through a video conferencing platform.
- The same holds true when friends move away or move to a different school. Be sure you exchange contact information, and keep these kids connected.

Working Through Friendship Challenges

Due to gifted perfectionism, a strong sense of fairness and justice, and gifted intensity, gifted children and adolescents can tend to walk away from friendships when they have felt let down or disappointed by the friend's actions. It can help to discuss this with your child if this happens for them. See if there is any possibility of rebuilding trust and friendship with the other friend. If so, find out what your child would need in order to take these steps, and help them practice stating what they need to their friend. Something simple like: *I like being your friend most of the time, but when you want to be in charge of everything we do, it is not fun for me. When you are ready to share this decision-making with me, let me know.* Talk with your child about your own experiences in this area.

If your child is still clear they wish to end the friendship, ask them if they might be willing to reconsider in a few months. Ask them if you can check back in with them to discuss after some time has passed, and do. Birthdays and other seasonal events can offer a natural way to revisit the issue.

Outgrown Friendships and Asynchrony

Another common gifted friendship dilemma I see in clients is when, due to asynchrony in development, gifted children and adolescents who were once close find they have little in common at various points in time. For example, two children may connect around certain interests—like a series of books or a popular video game—and one child outgrows the interest before the other. Other times, asynchrony in maturity levels occur.

It can be useful to talk about this directly with your children when you notice what may be happening. If they need a break from a friend, discuss their plan to do so. If a friend is taking a break from your child, honor and tend to any sadness your child might be feeling and discuss how to get through this time together.

You want to encourage your child by letting them know this is a natural part of growing up, and that there is a possibility that the two friends may find their way back to one another in the future. In my experience, it is usually best not to try to force the relationship to work but instead keep in touch in simple ways such as sending a Halloween card or a birthday well-wish. You can also use the opportunity to talk with your child about social concepts like bridge-burning.

Friendships with the Opposite Gender

Like young neurotypical children, young gifted boys and girls tend to befriend one another. But these friendships tend to hold steady well into elementary school, when neurotypical children can begin to group up by gender and gender roles. This dynamic can lead to misunderstanding and put pressure on gifted kids to explain the nature of their friendships. Gifted boys and girls may find it easier to just disengage from one another rather than face inaccurate accusations of a crush or love interest.

If your child is in this situation, I advise you to find ways to shelter and protect this connection for your child. This may mean inviting the other child to join your family in activities that will take the children out of the neighborhood and away from scrutiny, or private birthday lunches instead of invites to one another's birthday parties. Even with your support, the friendship may fade during late elementary and middle school. It can soothe your child to let them know there is a chance they may find a way back to this important friendship in high school or college.

BULLYING

Bullying is an unfortunate reality of any childhood, but sensitive gifted kids can be particularly at risk. In my experience, children who bully tend to do so because they have complicated and difficult lives, and they are discharging this pain in an attempt to feel more empowered. Humans in general tend to push on the people they feel safest with. When bullies target a child, it is often because that child is a safe target. It is almost as if the bully can gauge a gifted child's underlying sensitivity.

The longer a child is bullied, the more difficult it is to break the dynamic. When a gifted child I am working with has decided to address bullying, there are a few components that need to be put in place for a successful outcome:

① First, young people who are being bullied need to have some practice in speaking up for themselves in a clear, simple way. I usually suggest saying: *Stop*. Or, *I need you to stop*.

Gifted kids will often add in a *please* to the command to stop, something like: *Please, can you stop?* This kind of statement undermines the intention, because it actually gives the bully more power. Your child may need help finding and practicing their words.

② Second, parents need to be on board to debrief the new plan after school each day. It will take a few days to shift this dynamic, and it will become worse before it becomes better. Bullies not getting the same reaction they had received in the past will become louder, bigger, and meaner. You should make every effort to clear your after-school schedule to be with your child as they navigate this stretch of days. If this isn't possible, then plan to meet as soon as you can connect at the end of the day. Your child will need your support in this way.

③ Third, teachers and administrators need to be on board to support the gifted child in their efforts to change the bullying dynamic. The best way this can happen is if the teacher stays nearby, where the bullying tends to occur, and knows that the gifted child is planning to speak up to the bully. When the gifted child speaks up and the bully taunts further (*Oh, you need me to stop, make me stop.*) the teacher can step in out of the blue and say: *Sarah, I am confused. I heard Charlie say stop. Why didn't you stop?*

You will also need to gauge, in the spirit of safety, when your child needs additional support and assistance before implementing any kind of plan to shift a bullying dynamic. This is especially true in high school and with electronic or cyberbullying. You may need to discuss and plan with another authority like school administration or law enforcement.

④ Fourth, gifted children tend to understand who the bully will target next, after they break the bullying with them, and this can bring significant distress, as the gifted child may feel responsible for the next victim's pain. Gifted children will also have a sense of the pain the bully is experiencing underneath it all and may, on some level, feel conflicted. These responses are natural, and it is helpful to initiate conversations with your gifted child about these possibilities so they know that they have your support and feel less alone.

Bullying is a complicated matter that can be exceedingly difficult to resolve. I have suggested what I have seen work, but you may not have the support you need from school for the plan to be successful. You may also have a child who is a bully. I suggest you research more deeply the types and dynamics of bullying and victimhood. Barbara Coloroso's work in this area is a good place to start (see Resources on page 144).

Forgiveness and Apologies

We all know how a false apology feels. Sadly, it is often a practice in early education to ask children to apologize to one another before they are ready or before resolution has occurred, as part of conflict resolution. When this apology is feigned, it is like a second offense to a gifted child. Conversely, gifted children tend to be very hard on themselves, particularly after an incident where their intensity or perfectionism created a conflict with someone else. They can struggle to bounce back when they feel they have made a misstep or hurt a friend or family member.

Teaching a gifted child how to apologize and ask for forgiveness meaningfully can be a useful strategy to help them move on from an incident in which they feel they caused distress to someone.

At my office, I have had good results helping gifted people prepare to apologize or ask for forgiveness using a modified version of a model that I once heard Nobel laureate and Holocaust survivor Elie Wiesel discuss. It includes these components:

- When you are ready, name exactly what you did that merits apology to the person you harmed.
- Advise that you realize your action has caused them harm.
- If there was an awareness in advance that the action could potentially cause harm, admit you knew that when you took this action.
- Say you are sorry and ask the other person for forgiveness.

You will need to walk your child through these steps when they are ready and as they learn them. However, younger children and adolescents may only prepare using these steps, and their actual apology may be simpler. I recommend you use this same model, or another you prefer, as a template for apology and forgiveness within your home.

Authenticity and Power . . . Teach Relationship Dynamics

Throughout this book, we have explored relationship dynamics within gifted families and the parent-child relationship. For example, I continually suggest parents invest time in self-reflection to become clear about how their own experiences might influence how they parent, project upon, or experience their child.

This same process holds true within friendships, and in my practice I have noticed it is helpful for gifted young people to begin to get a sense of what they like or dislike in someone else, as it may actually be a reflection of something about themselves.

Additionally, triangulation (see sidebar in chapter 3) can be present within gifted friendships. It can be instructive for children to see how they might contribute to this dysfunction playing out within their friendships.

You may not feel comfortable approaching your child with these kinds of observations when you see them in their social interactions, but what you can do is earnestly address these same relational dilemmas within yourself and your relationships.

For example, if you notice your child has a mean competitive streak that can end a playdate in a moment, reflect on your own relationship with competition as well as your family culture.

▸ Do siblings compete for resources, attention, love, or bragging rights?

- ► How does this impact your child or the way your child interfaces with their school and friendship communities?
- ► What could change within yourself or the family culture that could ease this burden for your child?

Without calling attention to your efforts, becoming aware of these patterns may aid subtle shifts to occur, and this reflection may be enough to give space for your child to turn these corners as well. You can also begin these conversations directly with your child, especially if you struggle with the same issues, so you can name it and perhaps work together to change.

CHAPTER SEVEN

Making School Work

We've arrived at the final chapter, and the one that may hold the greatest interest to you as the parent of a gifted child: school. Understand from the start that this chapter is not about teaching you how to drill your gifted child into becoming an academic superstar. It is, instead, a guide to help you evaluate what works and what doesn't for your gifted child. This evaluation should hopefully be aided by the insights discussed in previous chapters. Understanding your child's true nature and temperament, as well as your role in shaping that, will help you navigate the challenges in the classroom. A miserable top-performing gifted student may struggle more in the long-term than an emotionally stable, fulfilled child with grades reflective of their love of learning within the right environment.

How to Choose the Right School

Every parent wants to find the right school and educator fit for their child. Yet, for a variety of reasons, this can be difficult to accomplish.

In my experience, the best school structure for gifted learners is a child-centered, or learner-centered approach. Child-centered philosophy follows and supports each learner's interests, while naturally and simultaneously fortifying self-development and a deep capacity to create meaningfully. Child-centered design trusts children's instincts and creativity so that intrinsic motivation naturally emerges.

Due to industrialization and later behavioral school influences on education and psychology, this humanistic, child-centered approach to learning has, with the exception of some homeschool and independent programs, all but vanished from our communities. Most learning today focuses on memorization mastery, grades, and performance. If you can find an environment or classroom educator weaving child-centered practices into their teaching, I suggest taking a close look for your gifted child.

Here are ideas on what to consider or ask as you select a school for your child:

- How will they engage my child in their learning?
- What stance do they take on competition in the learning environment?
- Will my child be expected to comply with authority here, or be free to establish meaningful relationships with their educators?
- How does this school encourage the development of intrinsic motivation?
- How will my child's advanced learning needs—including their capacity, pace, learning style, learning profile, interests, personality, and asynchrony—be differentiated and met every day?

- How will my child's other exceptionalities or challenges be seen, met, and supported every day? Will this educator or program see my child's exceptionalities as strengths, or as deficits?
- How do they establish and maintain social-emotional safety in the learning environment?
- What kinds of resources does this school offer my child beyond textbooks, worksheets, and packets?
- How will my child be expected to demonstrate learning? Homework? Testing? Is there openness to explore other options that may be more meaningful?
- In what ways will my child's advanced cognitive ability and creativity be nurtured and enriched in this environment?
- What process and timeline can I count on with this school for planning and implementing my child's advanced learning and support plans (see How to Create an Educational Plan on page 135)?
- How can the school detect whether my child is languishing? How will this be communicated to me? How will we address my child's needs not being met?

You will also need to ask each school for specific examples to illuminate how the school actually operates. It is easy for a school to say: *We offer differentiation and enrichment for our gifted learners.* Follow this statement up with: *Can you give us a few examples of how you tracked a gifted student's capacities and interests and used that to inform daily differentiation and enrichment offered to the child?* Ask each school to give you specific examples of how they provide what you are seeking. Do not let them off the hook; ask for specifics. If it becomes clear they cannot supply everything you are seeking, you are at least starting from a place of transparency and you can begin a timely exploration of how to meet these needs outside of school through finding a different school or homeschool, or arranging for tutors or other resources.

HOMESCHOOL OPTION

Homeschooling or unschooling is a great option and often necessary for gifted learners at some points in their education when a specific teacher or program year is not meeting their needs and it is affecting their learning or, worse, their emotional well-being. This is especially true for highly and profoundly gifted children.

Children who despair about going to school are candidates for homeschooling and unschooling. They are letting us know that school is unbearable. We have a responsibility to try to change or modify what isn't working, which, at the end of the day, can translate to homeschooling.

Regularly discuss with your child what is working (or not) in school to get a solid read on their well-being. Listen to their ideas about how they like to learn, who they like to learn from, and why. This longitudinal data will serve you and your child well if you decide at some point to homeschool so you can try to replicate the experiences that are working.

Parents rarely envision a reality where they are, on some level, homeschooling their children, and I understand what a shift in perspective it takes. However, homeschooling has come a long way and there are some workable modern developments to consider.

One strategy that works well for some of the gifted families I serve is forging a homeschool hybrid arrangement, where a child attends a traditional school part-time for what is meaningful to them—this might look like attending a science class with a beloved teacher, eating lunch with friends, and music class, then heading home for learning for the rest of the day.

To fill home learning needs, homeschool families can access creative online resources to learn almost every subject, although asking a child to work in a self-directed way at online school all day is unrealistic. There are homeschool collectives in different parts of the country where home-schooled gifted and twice-exceptional children and their parents can connect in person or online to access community and instruction, and parents can sometimes split any associated costs.

There is also a highly successful movement called radical unschooling that is beautifully child-centered, where children explore only what is interesting to them in real time, and parents support the process by checking in on what resources and access a child might need to deepen their learning—for example, arranging field trips or tracking down a scientist or other professional willing to meet online or answer a child's questions. Proponents of this model (correctly, in my opinion) believe that gifted children have an innate drive to learn and will and can learn what they need to know via this route.

I understand why parents might be skeptical of unschooling or radical unschooling. If the child is leading the learning, how can you ensure they will build the skills and develop the knowledge they need, particularly in subject content or skill development areas that are uninteresting to them, or are not their strengths? What is to keep them from playing video games all day? These are important questions. In response, I can offer that these intellectually curious children, if we can get out of their way, will seek out knowledge and explore in ways, and at a depth, we could not have constructed for them. Some natural skills development will sharpen in the process as children tend to their interests. Some skill development and content learning may need to be supplemented or woven in to meet state requirements or to prepare for future learning. Again, this is a discussion to have with your child. Say: *We have to add a bit of writing or math* to this subject. *How can we do this?* Listen to their ideas, brainstorm, and be creative together.

Even the process of unschooling lends itself to learning. I have helped families develop a simple process akin to preparing a research proposal, where gifted children meet regularly with their parents to present their ideas on what interests them next (see page 9). These child-led overviews naturally develop project and resource planning, collaboration and communication skills, perhaps requiring math, writing, critical thinking, and the scientific method. It helps to build skills like this naturally and move children closer to what they are interested in while they are young and motivated. Children will become self-aware around skills they wish to develop when they find something they want to learn or accomplish that requires a given skill. Let your child know you are there to help them access what they need. Plan together to support skill development, if possible, within their area of interest. You may find success by involving a mentor in the process of supporting learning and skill development. These methods can also align a child with ideas for what they want to achieve in life that may not have developed as easily. This is especially true for twice- or multi-exceptional children who feel defeated and sometimes "stupid" at school.

Not every family has the luxury of creating a homeschool configuration at a moment's notice, or at all. Yet I encourage you to stay open to the idea and seek out initial guidance within gifted parenting websites and forums. These parents are generally happy to share and help support new families. You will also need to check with your state in advance about homeschool guidelines you will be required to follow, including how to formally transition to homeschool and document and evaluate learning. I also suggest you regularly look at college policies on admission applications from homeschool students so you are working in that direction from the start. Again, getting resources from parents who homeschool in your community will help as you begin to understand what is expected of you. It is possible to balance work and put affordable homeschooling options together. If you do this homework now, you will be more prepared if it becomes clear it is necessary to quickly move your child out of a difficult learning situation.

Remember that homeschooling is not necessarily a permanent choice, but rather an option to be seriously considered and implemented when it could help your gifted child during a particular school year when factors like environmental or educator mismatch may be present.

Tips for Successful Teacher Meetings

It is important to forge a working relationship with your child's teacher. Education professionals are working in an era and atmosphere of extreme and unprecedented challenges within their field. There are school safety concerns and the stress of ongoing lockdowns and active shooter drills. Funding is tied to performance testing that requires creative teachers to focus on test readiness over student engagement. And, as I write, pandemic-related shifts have changed the landscape of the classroom to online teaching and remote learning. It is important to temper our goals of meeting a gifted child's learning needs with a spirit of collaboration, respect, and goodwill toward educators.

Here are recommendations for conferences and other conversations with teachers to make the most of your advocacy and collaboration.

- ▶ Be aware of your own experiences at your child's age and grade and remove any of your own educational wounding from the mix.
- ▶ Keep one notebook or file for each academic year and bring it to every meeting.
- ▶ Sketch out your concerns in advance of a meeting to keep your message clear.
- ▶ Prepare and bring along a written list of your questions.
- ▶ Keep your points succinct and listen closely.
- ▶ Pre-schedule follow-up meetings or communication to track progress and address related topics.
- ▶ Know your child's learning strengths and challenges.
- ▶ Sincerely listen to feedback about your child that is perhaps negative or contrary to what your child is telling you *without becoming defensive*. Check these discrepancies privately and kindheartedly with your child. Assure your child you understand, you have their back, and you will get through this together, but that honesty is important.
- ▶ Unless there's a safety concern, do not initially leapfrog over the educator to the administrator with concerns.
- ▶ Be prepared for misconceptions and misunderstandings about gifted and twice-exceptional learners. Do what you can to educate these educators. Try not to overwhelm them with material.
- ▶ Between conference meetings, resist sending lengthy or intense email messages to your child's teacher. Instead, write a brief email asking for a time to connect to discuss something you noticed.
- ▶ Let your child be part of the advocacy from the earliest age possible so they can understand how to have these

difficult but mature conversations. Once they are in high school, and certainly in college, you will have little to no voice in their advocacy, so help them be ready for this shift.

How to Create an Educational Plan

Gifted, twice-exceptional, and multi-exceptional children generally require additional support at school. Educational plans are part of that process. The first time you approach this planning, you will most likely feel overwhelmed. You are not alone. This section offers some general information, but state and district rules are particular so you will need to do some research about educational planning where you live. A valuable resource to help you advocate for your child is Barbara Jackson Gilman's book *Gifted Minds Empowered: Advocacy to Develop Gifted Children's Strengths* (2019).

There are protections, requirements, evaluation, and planning protocols for creating educational plans to provide the additional support a gifted child or twice-exceptional child may require. What is available to your family depends somewhat on your school setting (public or independent) and your state.

Parents generally carry the burden of initiating the plan process, which begins with a request for school evaluation and testing. Schools are required to respond and plan once a parent has initiated a request for an education plan, yet schools can delay in order to watch the child as a first response to a parent's request. This can slow down the process considerably, and you can request that the evaluation begins right away.

Parents may be asked for, or may wish to produce, documentation that could support the plan request, design, and implementation. This might include evaluations and recommendations from professionals who have worked with your child, like a pediatric occupational therapist, developmental optometrist, or a psychologist who provided IQ testing.

This planning process requires meetings with a team from your child's school, where you will discuss your child, their needs, evaluation reports from the school or your own team, and the school resources and responsibilities. The first time through the planning process can be tremendously confusing and stressful, as these meetings can feel overwhelmingly technical and cold. You can find a specialist—a consultant or educational attorney—to help you prepare for the meetings and possibly attend with you to clarify terms and your legal rights and to help you navigate the process, including directly challenging inconsistency or complacency.

Once plans are established, schools are required to implement the plan. In my experience, parents find they need to regularly track plan implementation and register concerns when a plan is not being followed. These plans continue to be revisited, reviewed, and updated, and they can also travel with a child to another school, sometimes including college. I recommend you take the responsibility to set up regularly scheduled plan reviews each academic year.

There are three types of plans to be aware of:

504 Plan

This plan name comes from Section 504 of the Rehabilitation Act of 1973, which is a civil rights law that prohibits any entity receiving federal funding from discriminating against individuals with disabilities.

If your child requires accommodations due to their disabilities, they are entitled to a 504 plan. Accommodations under a 504 plan are generally easy to implement—for example, giving a child more time on a test, providing a paper-and-pencil test versus an electronic test, seating in a certain part of the room, the ability to wear noise-canceling headphones while reading, or the ability to take stretch or sensory breaks during the day.

Individualized Education Plan (IEP)

This plan comes from the Individuals with Disabilities Education Act (IDEA), which requires accommodations that focus on specialized instruction and related services helpful to support learning when negotiating a learning disability. This type of plan requires schools provide much more in the way of instructional and services support, including specially designed instruction or individualized curriculum in one or more content subject areas. Be aware that although colleges offer assistance to students requiring support, the process is different. When you are considering college, ask each institution to walk you through how this works at their school.

Advanced Learning Plan Initiatives

Where I live and practice, schools are required by the state to create an individualized advanced learning plan for each gifted student. This stems from a law that defines exceptional children as "handicapped children, children with specific learning disabilities, and gifted children." Each state receiving funds under this law must produce a plan outlining how a free and appropriate education is available to exceptional children. Plans to support these learners vary between states.

Differentiation in the Classroom

It is thought to be helpful to provide gifted and twice-exceptional learners with differentiation in the classroom or school environment to meet their individual learning needs. This is often far easier said than done. This capacity can come naturally and easily for some school programs and educators, but can challenge other educators who are less supported by their districts, or who have not received meaningful training or resources in developing their practices. As author and giftedness advocate Barbara Jackson Gilman points out:

> ... even good teachers who try to meet all needs find that successful individualization is difficult, especially in large classes where student abilities range from the mildly delayed to the most highly gifted. (Gilman 2019)

Listed below are several ways schools or educators might attempt to support gifted learners. Keep in mind that differentiation is only helpful when it is working and is not causing other concerns. For your child's well-being, keep an eye out for what's working and what isn't. If your intuition is telling you something is off or not working for your child, advocate and speak up when you think a review or a change of practices is needed. It is important to stay firm, but respectful.

Acceleration is advancing a child to the next level of content learning where they have advanced capacity. This can happen within a subject or as a move to another grade level entirely. While you are considering acceleration, I think it is important to consider and plan for the social and emotional components of moving a younger asynchronous child into a classroom of older children; sometimes this works beautifully, and at other times it does not. You will need to be watchful of social and emotional dynamics and concerns.

Ability grouping is placing children together who are near one another in capacity, interests, or both, for learning and community. This might mean grouping children across different grades who are both gifted and neurotypical, who are pulled out of their classrooms to work together during the school day or week, or sometimes to join with another classroom session in progress. Schools that offer grouped gifted enrichment time during a school week are another example of ability grouping.

Advanced Placement or AP learning is seen in high school as a way to offer advanced material and methods to students in various subject content areas. Students are able, under certain conditions, to take some of this credit earned to college. This can sometimes backfire when a gifted student has acquired so much credit that they miss being placed in some first-year college courses, undercutting access to other first-year students and affecting their social-emotional experience.

Busywork is not a very evolved strategy and seems to be over-employed. A common example is increasing the quantity of work in a meaningless way for a gifted learner who has completed their work and needs something to do. Educators will supply more worksheets or more math problems reflecting material the student has already mastered. I advise you watch this closely in the early years and address it quickly.

Teacher Assistant. It is common for gifted children to be asked to help the teacher assist other students in an effort to keep them busy and also to support other, sometimes struggling, learners. This is a dangerous strategy for gifted learners, as it puts them at risk socially and emotionally in addition to taking them away from their own learning.

Self-Advocacy

As you work to advocate for your child, it is also important to help your gifted child learn steps to advocate for themselves as well. If children haven't had practice in self-advocacy when younger, they can be reluctant to self-advocate as they become older. This is problematic for everyone, because as a parent you will have less access and voice as an advocate for a high school student. Start small—listen to their laments and help them find a place to start. Maybe this is requesting a teacher review a math concept privately with them. Or maybe they have already read the book the class is reading and they wish to read something else. Maybe they have an alternative idea for a project. Help your child prepare and practice what they wish to say to their teacher.

PERSONAL LEARNING STORIES TO EXPLORE

There is much to do to support gifted and twice-exceptional children and teens in their evaluation, learning, and well-being. It can feel overwhelming to obtain the evaluative and procedural information you need and then to find and use your own authentic advocacy voice, all within the context of loving your child. I find it can be helpful for parents to be aware of and access the inspirational work of brilliant individuals who have written or spoken about their own difficult educational or life paths, or the paths of others, and the supports that assisted them to move through their education and life experience to grounded accomplishment. Discovering these stories may help you feel empowered and better able to set your advocacy compass. Here are some stories I find inspiring:

- **L. Todd Rose,** author of *Square Peg: My Story and What It Means for Raising Innovators, Visionaries, and Out-of-the Box Thinkers,* describes his path and what supports helped him move from a difficult childhood to high school dropout to Harvard educator.

- **Jonathan Mooney and David Cole,** authors of *Learning Outside the Lines: Two Ivy League Students with Learning Disabilities and ADHD Give You the Tools for Academic Success and Educational Revolution,* give us ways to understand how to move beyond the damage that can occur within institutionalized education and succeed on our own terms, with our hearts intact. These groundbreakers also created a legendary program called Eye-to-Eye (see Resources) for youths with learning challenges. Mr. Mooney has authored other excellent related books you will find listed in the Resources section.

- **Scott Barry Kaufman,** author of *Ungifted: Intelligence Redefined, The Truth About Talent, Practice, Creativity, and the Many Paths to Greatness,* from an accomplished and scholarly position, gives a sweeping overview of intelligence, including some key challenges within the field of gifted and talented education, ignited by his childhood story of placement in special education and eventual placement in gifted programming.

- **Diana Beresford-Kroeger,** author of *To Speak for the Trees: My Life's Journey From Ancient Celtic Wisdom to a Healing Vision of the Forest,* shares the interesting route and experiences bringing her into work as a prominent scientist, born from childhood tragedy.

- **Storyteller Steve Zimmer** gives a poignant account of his young experience of trying to keep afloat in first grade in his audio story *Stars, Rockets, and Moons*, available at TheMoth.org.

▸ **Ken Robinson and Lou Aronica,** authors of *The Element: How Finding Your Passion Changes Everything*, give us sketches of extraordinary lives emerging from a variety of circumstances.

· ·

Conclusion

It has been my honor to be with you on this part of your gifted journey. If we were meeting in my practice in my Boulder, Colorado office, you might know how I end every counseling meeting with children, adolescents, teens, and their families: with an appreciation circle. Everyone shares one thing they love or appreciate about everyone else in the room. My appreciations tend to be long-winded and a bit of therapy-speak. Sometimes I even get a tiny bit tearful as I acknowledge a gifted youngster who has worked courageously to truly create the life they wish for themself.

Since we are not at my office, I will need to communicate my appreciation to you here:

I appreciate . . .

. . . your dedication to better understand your gifted child.

. . . your openness in reading through and considering some of the challenging directives I sent your way, particularly all of the self-reflection.

. . . it is not so easy to make changes, and your exploration here is perhaps a brave, and certainly a caring, step.

. . . your willingness to try to see, and perhaps offset, the unnecessary challenges gifted children, adolescents, teens, adults, and families face.

And, I appreciate . . .

. . . your commitment to parent and support a gifted child to find their way well in this world.

I said in the beginning, be true to yourself as you navigate this material. I meant it. Take what works for you and leave the rest. At the end of this book you will find references and resources to take you on from here. Trust yourself as you take these next noble steps in your parenting journey.

Resources

ASYNCHRONY

Giftedness 101 by Linda Kreger Silverman

Off the Charts: Asychrony and the Gifted Child by Christine Neville, Michael M. Piechowski, and Stephanie S. Tolan

Mellow Out, They Say. If I Only Could: Intensities and Sensitivities of the Young and Bright by Michael M. Piechowski

DABROWSKI

Dabrowski's Theory of Positive Disintegration by Sal Mendaglio

Positive Disintegration by Kazimierz Dabrowski

Living with Intensity by Susan Daniels and Michael M. Piechowski

Website with original works:

www.positivedisintegration.com

EMPATHIC NATURE

Positive Energy: 10 Extraordinary Prescriptions for Transforming Fatigue, Stress & Fear, Into Vibrance, Strength & Love by Judith Orloff

GIFTED ORGANIZATIONS

Gifted Development Center

www.gifteddevelopment.org

Hoagies' Gifted Education Page

www.hoagiesgifted.org

National Association for Gifted Children

www.nagc.org

Supporting the Emotional Needs of the Gifted

www.sengifted.org

HOMESCHOOL

Gifted Homeschool Forum

www.ghflearners.org

MINDFULNESS

FocusedKids
www.focusedkids.org

Mindfulness Coloring Book for Kids ... with Guidance for Those Who Love Them by Kathy Hegberg

FocusedKids Mini Book of Mindful Exercises: Supporting Self-Regulation in Young Children by Kathy Hegberg

FamiliasFocalizadas con FocusedKids?: Actividades Conscientes Basadas en el Cerebro para Mejorar la Autoregulacion en Ninos y Adultos (Spanish Edition) by Kathy Hegberg

The Mindful Child by Susan Kaiser Greenland

PARENTING

Unconditional Parenting: Moving from Rewards and Punishments to Love and Reason by Alfie Kohn

PERFECTIONISM

Meeting at the Crossroads: Women's Psychology and Girls' Development by Lyn Mikel Brown and Carol Gilligan

Perfectionism: A Practical Guide to Managing "Never Good Enough" by Lisa Van Gemert

POLYVAGAL THEORY

Beyond Behaviors: Using Brain Science and Compassion to Understand and Solve Children's Behavior by Mona Delahooke,

The Pocket Guide to the Polyvagal Theory by Stephen W. Porges

Stephen Porges Website

www.stephenporges.com

SCHOOL

The Bully, The Bullied, and the Not-So-Innocent Bystander by Barbara Colorosa

Creative Writing Solutions (Druidawn) Website

www.creative-writing-solutions.com

Doing Poorly on Purpose: Strategies to Reverse Underachievement and Respect Student Dignity by James R. Delisle

The Power of Self-Advocacy for Gifted Learners: Teaching The Essential Four Steps to Success by Deb Douglas

Gifted Minds Empowered: Advocacy to Develop Gifted Children's Strengths by Barbara Jackson Gilman

Punished by Rewards: The Trouble with Gold Stars, Incentive Plans, A's, Praise, and Other Bribes by Alfie Kohn

Creative Schools: The Grassroots Revolution That's Transforming Education by Ken Robinson and Lou Aronica

Learning Outside the Lines by Jonathan Mooney and David Cole

Virtues Project Website

www.virtuesproject.org

TWICE-EXCEPTIONALITY

AbleKids Foundation (Central Auditory Processing Disorder)

www.ablekidsfoundation.org

Dyslexic Advantage Website

www.dyslexicadvantage.org

The Dyslexic Advantage: Unlocking the Hidden Potential of the Dyslexic Brain by Brock & Fernette Eide

Eye to Eye Organization Website

www.eyetoeyenational.org

Twice Exceptional: Supporting and Educating Bright and Creative Students with Learning Difficulties by Scott Barry Kaufman

Your Child's Vision: A Parent's Guide to Seeing, Growing and Developing by Richard S. Kavner

Different Minds: Gifted Children with AD/HD, Asperger Syndrome, and Other Learning Deficits by Dierdre Lovecky

Sensational Kids: Hope and Help for Children with Sensory Processing Disorder by Lucy Jane Miller, Doris A. Fuller, and Janice Rotenberg

Learning Outside the Lines: Two Ivy League Students with Learning Disabilities and ADHD Give You the Tools for

Academic Success and Educational Revolution by Jonathan Mooney and David Cole

Normal Sucks: How to Live, Learn, and Thrive Outside the Lines by Jonathan Mooney

The Short Bus: A Journey Beyond Normal by Jonathan Mooney

Giftedness 101 by Linda Kreger Silverman

The 2e Resource Website

www.2eresource.com

VISUAL SPATIAL LEARNING

Upside-Down Brilliance: The Visual-Spatial Learner by Linda Kreger Silverman

References

Baumrind, Diana. 1967. "Child Care Practices Anteceding Three Patterns of Preschool Behavior." Genetic Psychology Monographs 75: 43-88.

Betts, George T. and Jolene K. Kercher. 1999. *Autonomous Learner Model: Optimizing Ability* Model. Greeley, Colo.: ALPS Pub.

Betts, G. T., and Neihart, M. (2010). "Revised profiles of the gifted and talented." Retrieved September 1, 2020, from https://sciencetalenter.dk/sites/default/files/revised_profiles _of_the_gifted_and_talented_-_neihart_and_betts.pdf.

Betts, George T., Robin J Carey, and Blanche M. Kapushion. 2016. *Autonomous Learner Model Resource Book.*

Betts, George T., and Maureen Neihart. 1988. "Profiles of the Gifted and Talented." *Gifted Child Quarterly* 32 (2): 248-253. doi:10.1177/001698628803200202.

Bowen, Murray. 1966. "The Use of Family Theory in Clinical Practice." *Comprehensive Psychiatry* 7 (5): 345-374. doi:10.1016/s0010-440x(66)80065-2.

Bowen, Murray. 2004. *Family Therapy in Clinical Practice.* Lanham, Md.: Rowman & Littlefield.

Dąbrowski, K. 1964. *Positive Disintegration.* Boston, Mass.: Little, Brown.

Dąbrowski, Kazimierz, Andrzej Kawczak, and Michael M Piechowski. 1970. *Mental Growth Through Positive Disintegration.* London: Gryf Publications.

Daniels, Susan, and Michael M Piechowski Eds. 2009. *Living with Intensity.* Scottsdale, AZ: Great Potential Press.

Delisle, James R. 2018. *Doing Poorly on Purpose: Strategies to Reverse Underachievement and Respect Student Dignity.* ASCD.

Gilman, Barbara Jackson. 2019. *Gifted Minds Empowered: Advocacy to Develop Gifted Children's Strengths*. pp 352. Broomfield, CO: EmpowerOne Publishing.

Gross, Miraca U. M. 1993. *Exceptionally Gifted Children*. Routledge.

Gross, Miraca. 2001. ""Play Partner" or "Sure Shelter"? Why Gifted Children Prefer Older Friends." Presentation, 4th Australian International Confernce on the Education of Gifted Students, 2001.

Guerney, Bernard. 1964. "Filial Therapy: Description and Rationale." *Journal of Consulting Psychology* 28 (4): 304-310. doi:10.1037/h0041340.

Guerney, Louise F., and Virginia Ryan. 2013. *Group Filial Therapy: The Complete Guide to Teaching Parents to Play Therapeutically with Their Children*. London: Jessica Kingsley Publishers.

Hegberg, Kathy. 2002. Personal communication.

Hendrix, Harville, and Helen Hunt. 2019. *Getting the Love You Want: A Guide for Couples*. 3rd ed. St. Martin's Griffin.

Hollingworth, Leta Stetter. 1926. *Gifted Children: Their Nature and Nurture* (Experimental Education Series). MacMillan.

Individuals with Disabilities Education Improvement Act of 2004, Pub. L. 108-446 (formerly Education for All Handicapped Children Act of 1975, Pub. L. No. 94-142).

Jung, Carl. 1939. *The Integration of the Personality*, 1st ed., 285. Farrar & Rinehart, Inc.

Jung, Carl. 1979. "Chapter Three: Shadow." In *Aion: Researches into the Phenomenology of the Self,* 2nd ed. pp. 285. Princeton University Press.

Jung, Carl. 2014. "Introversion/Extraversion." In *Collected Works of C.G. Jung*, Volume 6: Psychological Types, 3rd ed., 60-87. Princeton University Press.

Karpinski, Ruth, Kinase Kolb, Tetreault, and Borowski. 2018. "High Intelligence: A Risk Factor for Psychological and Physiological Overexcitabilities." *Intelligence* 66: 8-23.

Karpman M.D., and Stephen B. 2014. *A Game Free Life: The New Transactional Analysis of Intimacy, Openness, and Happiness*. San Francisco: Drama Triangle Publications.

Karpman M.D., and Stephen B. 2019. *Collected Papers In Transactional Analysis*. San Francisco: Drama Triangle Publications.

Kavner, Richard S. 1985. *Your Child's Vision: A Parent's Guide To Seeing, Growing and Developing*. New York: Simon and Schuster.

Kerr, Barbara A. 1985. "Smart Girls, Gifted Women: Special Guidance Concerns." *Roeper Review* 8 (1): 30-33. doi:10.1080/02783198509552923.

Kohn, Alfie. 1993. *Punished by Rewards: The Trouble with Gold Stars, Incentive Plans, A's, Praise, and Other Bribes*. Houghton Mifflin Harcourt Trade & Reference Publishers.

Kohn, Alfie. 2005. *Unconditional Parenting: Moving from Rewards and Punishments to Love and Reason*. New York: Atria Books.

Lovecky, Deirdre V. 1998. "Spiritual Sensitivity in Gifted Children." *Roeper Review* 20 (3): 178-183. doi:10.1080/02783199809553887.

Mann, Horace. 1957. "How Real Are Friendships of Gifted and Typical Children in a Program of Partial Segregation?" *Exceptional Children* 23 (5): 199-201. doi:10.1177/001440295702300502.

Marland, S.P. 1972. *Education of the Gifted and Talented (Report to the Subcommittee on Education, Committee on Labor and Public Welfare, U.S. Senate)*. Ebook. Washington D.C.: US Government Printing Office. https://www.valdosta.

edu/colleges/education/human-services/document%20/
marland-report.pdf.

Mayer, John D., Donna M. Perkins, David R.
Caruso, and Peter Salovey. 2001. "Emotional Intelligence and Giftedness". *Roeper Review* 23 (3): 131-137.
doi:10.1080/02783190109554084.

Mendaglio, Sal. 2008. *Dabrowski's Theory of Positive Disintegration.* Scottsdale, AZ: Great Potential Press.

Miller, Lucy J., Doris A. Fuller, and Janice Roetenberg.
2014. *Sensational Kids: Hope and Help for Children with Sensory Processing Disorder.* TarcherPergiree

Mooney, Jonathan, and David Cole. 2000. *Learning Outside the Lines.* New York: Simon & Schuster.

National Association for Gifted Children. 2019. *A Definition of Giftedness That Guides Best Practice.* Ebook. https://
www.nagc.org/sites/default/files/Position%20Statement/
Definition%20of%20Giftedness%20%282019%29.pdf.

Neville, Christine S., Michael M. Piechowski, and Stephanie S. Tolan, eds. 2013. *Off the Charts: Asynchrony and the
Gifted Child.* Unionville, NY: Royal Fireworks Press.

No Child Left Behind Act of 2001. Pub. L. 107-110.

O'Shea, Harriet E. 1960. "Friendship and the Intellectually Gifted Child." *Exceptional Children* 26 (6): 327-335.
doi:10.1177/001440296002600605.

Perfect, Michelle M., Matt R. Turley, John S. Carlson,
Justina Yohanna, and Marla Pfenninger Saint Gilles. 2016.
"School-Related Outcomes of Traumatic Event Exposure
and Traumatic Stress Symptoms in Students: A Systematic
Review of Research from 1990 To 2015." *School Mental Health*
8 (1): 7-43. doi:10.1007/s12310-016-9175-2.

Perry, B.D. 2002. "Childhood Experience and the Expression of Genetic Potential: What Childhood Neglect Tells Us
About Nature and Nurture." *Brain and Mind* 3: 79-100.

Piechowski, Michael M. 1979. Chapter: Developmental Potential. In N. Colangelo & R.T. Zaffrann (Eds.), *New Voices in Counseling the Gifted*. Dubuque, Iowa: Kendall/Hunt.

Piechowski, Michael M. 2003. Chapter: Emotional and Spiritual Giftedness. pp 413. In Colangelo, Nicholas, et al (Eds.) *Handbook of Gifted Education*. 3rd ed. Boston: Allyn and Bacon.

Piechowski, Michael M. 2014. *Mellow Out, They Say. If I Only Could: Intensities and Sensitivities of the Young and Bright*. Unionville, NY. Royal Fireworks Press.

Plucker, Burroughs, and Song. 2010. *Mind the (Other) Gap: The Growing Excellence Gap in K-12 Education*. Ebook. Center for Evaluation & Education Policy. https://files.eric.ed.gov/fulltext/ED531840.pdf.

Pollack, William S. 1999. *Real Boys*. Melbourne, Victoria: Scribe Publications.

Porges, Stephen W. 2017. *The Pocket Guide to the Polyvagal Theory: The Transformative Power of Feeling Safe*. New York: W. W. Norton & Company.

Rehabilitation Act of 1973. Pub. L. 93-112.

Renzulli, Joseph S. 2005. "The Three-Ring Conception of Giftedness: A Developmental Model for Promoting Creative Productivity." *Conceptions of Giftedness*, 246-279. doi:10.1017/cbo9780511610455.015.

Rivero, Lisa. 2010. *A Parent's Guide to Gifted Teens*. Scottsdale, AZ: Great Potential Press.

Rivero, Lisa. 2010. *The Smart Teens Guide to Living with Intensity*. Tuscon, AZ: Great Potential Press.

Robinson, Ken, and Lou Aronica. 2015. *Creative Schools: The Grassroots Revolution That's Transforming Education*. New York: Penguin Publishing Group.

Roeper, Annemarie. 1982. "How the Gifted Cope with Their Emotions." *Roeper Review* 5 (2): 21-24. doi:10.1080/02783198209552672.

Silverman, L.K. 1992, (Jan.- Feb.). "From the Editor." *Understanding Our Gifted*, 4 (3), 2.

Silverman, L.K. (ed.). 1993. "The Gifted Individual." In *Counseling the Gifted and Talented*. (pp. 3-28). Denver, CO: Love.

Silverman, L.K. 1997. "A Construct of Asynchronous Development." *Peabody Journal of Education*, 72 (3&4) 36-58.

Silverman, Linda Kreger. 2002. *Upside-Down Brilliance: The Visual-Spatial Learner*. Denver, Colo.: DeLeon Pub.

Silverman, Linda Kreger. 2013a. *Giftedness 101*. New York: Springer.

Silverman, Linda Kreger. 2013b. "Asynchronous Development: Theoretical Bases in Current Applications." *Off the Charts: Asynchrony and the Gifted Child*. Eds. Neville, Piechowski and Tolan. Unionville, NY: Royal Fireworks Press..

Silverman, Linda. 2018. "Assessment of Giftedness." In *Handbook of Giftedness in Children*, 183-207. New York: Springer.

Silverman, Linda. (in press). "Counseling Asynchronous Gifted Students: A Thirty-Year Perspective." Tracy L. Cross and Jennifer Riedl Cross, eds. In *Handbook for School Counselors Serving Students with Gifts & Talents*, 2nd ed. Waco, TX: Prufrock Press.

Washington, Harriet A. 2019. *A Terrible Thing to Waste: Environmental Racism and Its Assault on the American Mind*. Little, Brown Spark.

Index

Acknowledgments

I wish to acknowledge...

Kathy Hegberg for helping me find the path and authenticity of my work.

Meg Harrison for showing me how to see and include the brilliant glimmer in the gravity of this work.

Members of my Dabrowski Study Group—especially Chris Wells, Michael Piechowski, and Kathee Jones—for their manuscript suggestions and in helping me clarify my reference points and voice.

Linda Silverman, Bobbie Gilman, Nancy Miller, Frank Falk, and the exceptional team of professionals at Gifted Development Center in Denver for their pioneering work supporting gifted children and families, and for helping me to find my way in the field.

Steve Higgins for writing the book foreword, and for not being gifted.

My kindergarten teachers Mrs. McDade and Mrs. Malone, for preparing me, through their everyday creativity, kindness, and integrity, to be better able to work well with children.

My high school dean Jane Peterson, for being an excellent influence on my life.

My dear family for the love, fun, kindness, learning, and support aboard the SS Happiness Is....

About the Author

Catherine Zakoian, MA, NCC, LPC, is a national-board certified and licensed professional counselor in the Rocky Mountains of Colorado. Her private counseling practice, www.catherinezakoian.com, offers individual and family counseling services for gifted, twice-exceptional (2e), and profoundly gifted children, adolescents, teens, adults, families, and organizations. Her educational consultation practice provides steadfast guidance on creating psychologically healthful educational environments, authentic leadership and program development, and meaningful educator self-awareness and care within well-recognized public, independent, and alternative preK–12 programs and schools serving gifted and neurotypical populations. She has presented regionally, nationally, and internationally on giftedness.